Mantras, Yantras & Fabulous Gems

the healing secrets of the ancient Vedas

by
Howard Beckman
Copywright 1996

© 1996 Howard Beckman
Balaji Publishing Co.
First hardback edition 1997

Front cover painting
"Root Mantra of Goddess of Wealth"
by Acharya Ram Charan Sharma 'Vyakul'

ISBN O 9525172 5 6
A British Library catalogue record is available for this book.

Printed and bound in Great Britain by
ChandlersPrinters

DEDICATION

I dedicate this book to my spiritual master His Divine Grace A.C. Bhaktivedanta Swami Prabhupada by whose infinite mercy I have gained some appreciation of the Vedas and of the goal of self-realisation. May this book serve as a springboard for others to gain some enthusiasm toward understanding the journey of the eternal soul.

My heartfelt thanks to all who encouraged and helped in the production of this book. A special thank you to Mike Wright for once again taking his valuable time to do the initial editing, and to Lynwen Crowley for having the perseverence to enter all Mike's changes into the computer. Once again Raju Nandha has donated his time and superb skills in taking all the photographs of gemstones and Yantras, and for this I am forever grateful. Also my appreciation to Steven Moser for all the hand drawings of yantras, as well as the chakras.

The final edit was done thanks to the love of Liz Gibson, who did it even while having her own work on overload.

Finally to my wife Jennifer who has beat me over the head to get this and my last book out, and has done more to help me than I could ever repay. To have such a faithful, loving partner is rare in this world, and I thank her with all my heart.

TABLE OF CONTENTS

FORWARD

This book by Howard Beckman (Hamsavatar das) is an important work for western students of vedic science. We believe it will also be very helpful to the second and third generations of those of Indian lineage born in western countries to understand the secret spiritual sciences of their ancestors. Although simplified to some extent, especially in the sections on mantra and yantra, it gives a basic knowledge of these subjects to those not interested in making too indepth a study. The planetary section is as complete as any practicing astrologer could hope for, therefore it will give the general public a very thorough understanding of the science of gemstone therapy used in vedic astrology and ayurvedic medicine.

For the student wishing to study in detail the "Tantra", it serves as a first step to understanding the powers of sound vibration in mantra and yantra, as well as the meaning of their installation, worship, and formation. More than anything the reader gets the feeling of committment on the part of the author to his own study and practice of these arts and sciences.

In this last decade of the twentieth century many fads and trends from fashion to language and philosophy use some portion of vedic science incorporated into western lifestyle. There are so many different groups of persons giving their own views of what they mean, but these sciences must be understood as they were originally presented to be effectual. Our feeling is that this book will be recognised as the work of a man who is a true devotee of not only vedic science, but the overall spiritual culture of ancient India. To hear such knowledge presented "as it is", without change, will give those of us wading through the deep waters of these subjects a guide with which to begin our journey.

The Publishers

INTRODUCTION

My purpose in writing this book is to present some bona-fide information on the science of healing through vibration of sacred vedic mantras, mathematically and geometrically perfect yantras and the use of natural gemstones as delineated in the vedic scriptures of ancient India. So much information abounds in the marketplace, yet much of it (now called New-Age) is without a common or reliable source in which the reader can have faith.

Most of the information on vedic mantra and yantra are in Indian publications which are difficult for the average westerner to comprehend as they are written with the premise that the reader already has some basic or fundamental knowledge of the subject matter. There are some texts written in English on gemstone therapy yet my wife and I searched in vain when researching this book to find any books encompassing all three of these subjects. We travelled all over India, researching books in stores, libraries, and museums. We not only found nothing which contained these subjects together, but found very few that the average westerner would read past the first page due to the style of writing being aimed solely at those of Indian background and culture.

The texts found in the west on gem therapy and the medicinal use of gemstones rarely agree in their conclusions and seem to have no real bona-fide sources for coming to them. The texts of the other civilisations known to have such knowledge many thousands of years ago have long since disappeared. There are no authoritative texts which predate the sanskrit vedic texts of ancient India. These vedas are said to be the authority and law books for mankind, being of divine descent. Almost everything I could find written by westerners which wasn't based on the vedic version was inconclusive and speculative. There was disagreement as to the actual potencies of the gems, as well as how they could be used. Most were considered "folklore" and even the authors themselves seemed unconvinced as to the efficacy of what they were writing about.

Some of the books written in the most recent years were said to be "channelled" information, that a being of higher knowledge and "channelled" information, that a being of higher knowledge and consciousness, no longer dwelling on the physical plane of existence, spoke it using the body of a medium to communicate through. Although this is nothing new or astounding still there should be a verifiable source for such information, which thus far has not been found.

I am hopeful that those who take the time to read this book will find it informative and helpful in understanding the purpose and uses of mantras, yantras and gems in healing the body, mind, and spirit. My even greater hope is that the readers will gain some insight into their own needs and desires on a higher plane of spiritual consciousness, causing them to further delve into higher truths available within the texts of the ancient vedic civilisation.

SOUND VIBRATION

Before going into mantras, which are sacred sound vibrations, it's important to understand the source from which they are born, namely sound, or sound vibration. From one vibration comes another and thus all motion creates further motion and all activity creates more activity. To perceive gradations of sound vibration we must begin from a position of silence, within and without.

Different gradations of vibrational activity are what account for the various planes of existence. There are many other worlds beyond this one and there are other dimensions of the world we live in not visible to most humans with our gross senses. Different worlds are coexisting simultaneously, yet still within one sphere. There are also various other dimensional planes of life existing on a subtle level, like those worlds inhabited by disembodied living entities(ghosts). Additionally there exist purely mental planes, but in all there is life of an advanced intellectual and/or spiritual nature. Some of us are sensitive enough to perceive such other dimensions existing around us, yet most people's senses are far too blunted, even psychically, to have any awareness.

We are constantly surrounded by vibrations, within and without. All which we perceive depends upon vibration, in our thinking, feeling and willing ourselves into consequent actions. It is how we direct our actions which accounts for the many varieties of life, be it on the physical or the subtle planes of existence, in this world or another. How we direct our actions in this life directly develops the opportunity for action in future lives. In other words every action begets an equal or greater reaction. This is known generally as the law of karma.

There are various degrees of vibrations, both subtle (thought) and gross (physical). The elements came into order one after another. First there was sound, and from sound the ether was generated. From ether came the air. When there is friction in the air, fire (electricity) is created. From excessive heat, water is then generated, as we can see that the rainy season follows the hot summer season. From water comes the earth.

Each element has its characteristics and attributes. Thus all the elements are generated sequentially and the bodies of all living beings are comprised of these elements. We perceive some vibrations with our physical eyes and senses. These vibrations are those of matter, comprised of atoms and made up of the elements of earth, water, fire, air and ether. Higher subtle vibrations are perceived by the mind, which are on the plane of thought. Higher still are the vibrations of feelings, perceived by the soul. The finest or most subtle vibrations are not even perceived by the individual soul, yet it is these vibrations which comprise the immutable, eternal soul, our "true self".

Vibration causes differentiations as a result of the driving forces; for example in sound, the difference in force causes variations in the tone, whereas on the atomic, physical level variations cause colour change. In the activity of being conscious, a state also driven by vibration, sound teaches us to know ourselves, or in other words the consciousness witnesses the outer self through the voice. Sound is within all things and is, therefore, the origin of all things. Any motion will create sound which is stored hidden within it. Different sounds may be perceived as harmonious or disharmonious and therefore sound can also be healing for the mind and body. All things and all beings have a distinct tone or sound according to their level of evolution. There have been many advances, even in modern day, of using tones, sound vibrations of a specific pitch and intensity, to promote healing on a physical, as well as subtle level.

Planets each have their resonant tone and the earth planet in particular has varieties of sound, as well as colour. Stringed and all percussion instruments represent the sound of earth and the colour is yellow. These sounds produce movement of the body.

The deep sound of water is heard in running streams or any moving body of water including the sound of rain. Its colour is green and these sounds have very definite effects upon emotions and imagination. The sound of fire is of a very high frequency and of red colour. It may be perceived in sound as that of thunder or a volcanic eruption. The sound of air may be perceived in the blowing of the wind and stormy weather. The effect is piercing to the heart and may be expressed through all wind instruments, be they made of metal, wood or bamboo, chief of which is the flute. The sound of air is a "living" sound, thus overpowering all others. Its influence brings joy and ultimately ecstasy. The sound of ether is self-contained and is the origin of all others. Its resonance is unending, all-pervading, yet it is not audible to the ear. The body becomes the instrument, once purified of all material contamination. The ultimate effect is knowledge, revelation, fearlessness and unending joy. In the materially afflicted state it causes weakness and abnormalities of the body and/or mind. Only those who elevate their consciousness through spiritual practice can become elevated through the vibration of the ether.

The combinations of these sounds have varied effects on living beings. Earth-water sounds together are delicate and have a tenderness about them. The sound of earth-fire is harsh and grating. That of earth-air is powerful and strong; that of water-fire alive and animated. Sounds of water-ether are soothing and calming, while that of fire-air produce fear and terror. Sounds of fire-ether give a feeling of freedom whilst that of air-ether create peace and tranquillity.

The original state of the soul is one of joyfulness and peace. This vibration of the spirit soul is of the finest essence whilst that for external matter of the grossest. All life is eternal, being made of spirit and all matter is temporary, subject to change and destruction. It is due to man's absorption in the affairs of transient matter, destined to be destroyed, that he is deluded and his true nature as spirit covered.

There are innumerable vibrational combinations of both spirit and matter, yet from the same source. Within the cells of our own bodies are living many tiny living entities. Indeed on all planes of our existence there are living entities born of and living within other living entities. There are many living germs and microbes within the gross, physical body that are born of it. Likewise there are living entities born of our thoughts and, although their existence is finer than those born of the body, they exist all the same. As germs live in our physical bodies, other living entities live within our mental planes. Thoughts also have life, even more so than the physical, and go through birth, ageing and death processes. According to their nature they become an advantage or disadvantage to our evolution.

Vibrations also have size and strength. Our spoken words will only reach the ears of those listening, while the vibration of thought reaches a far greater distance from one mind to another. The feelings and emotions of the heart can enter the hearts of others, allowing them to feel within their hearts what we are feeling within our own. The soul vibrations are of the greatest power and highest frequency, and easily connect one with another. In all conditions of life and on all planes of existence there is a connection through vibration. Have you ever noticed how one person coughing or yawning in a room of people will cause others to do the same? Laughter is also infectious and we easily convey our feelings of happiness or depression similarly through vibrations, not the spoken words. Therefore a person who has the "eyes to see" on an inner level is called a spiritual "seer". Such gifted people can know all things past, present and future on all planes of existence.

There is a sympathy in vibration between humans, other living beings and our surroundings. Have you ever heard of a dog's howl telling of a death to come, or horses' neighing warning of imminent danger? Not only animals but also plant-life will be affected through this vibrational bond. In times of sadness and sorrow plants and flowers may die, while they flourish in times of upliftment and happiness.

We become bereft of the ability to perceive these vibrations in accordance with the development of our ego. This "false egoism" is what blinds us. There is a "real ego", but this remains unknown unless and until seekers uncover their actual eternal and original "identity". This is different to those which are temporary and perceived according to the present bodily identification. Vibrations are everywhere and their influences are left wherever people have been. This is how a "psychic" or clairvoyant can pick up a person's vibrations from an article of clothing or from entering a room.

Our vibrations depend on which modes of nature most affect us. This could range from the mode of goodness (sattva), the mode of passion (rajas), to the mode of ignorance or darkness (tamas). We live in various combinations of these modes of nature and only when purified to the point of living in complete goodness may we finally move on to the point of true spiritual life and realisation. This is the point of "transcendence" above and beyond the modes and worlds of material nature. Therefore those purified of the affectations of these material modes, situated in transcendence and known as a "seer", can tell from a person's vibration what consciousness has been developed, just as a musician can understand what key a song is being played in simply by hearing it.

There are three basic waking levels of consciousness. Unfortunately most people experience only two. Primarily there is sensual consciousness where we rely on our physical senses for all perception and fulfillment of perceived desires. On this level we are no different than animals as everything revolves around satisfying the physical senses of the body. The concerns are basic. Eating, sleeping, sexual desires and the fear of losing material acquisitions and thus defend what we mistakenly believe to be "ours".

Beyond the sensual level of consciousness is the intellectual level. Most of us also dwell on this level which involves the mind's always accepting or rejecting things as good or bad, desirable or undesirable. We speculate and intellectualise over the mechanisms of the material world including that which is far beyond our ability to experiment. Just like the scientists of present day who make so many speculations about the origin of life and the creation of the universe. Their evaluations are simply unfounded speculations for there is no way of experimenting with that which lies beyond the purview of their senses. The speculative theory that life comes from chemicals has always been and forever continues to be an absurdity. Otherwise why can't these scientists mix together chemicals to produce life? It is impossible for life comes from life, not chemicals. The living principle within the material body is the immutable, imperishable spirit soul. When the soul is present, we perceive the body to be alive. When the soul has left the body, we perceive the body to be dead. Scientists have been able to mix ovum from a female and sperm from a male to allow conception to take place within a test-tube, but they cannot chemically produce ovum or sperm. The reason the conception takes place is because within each spermatozoa is a spirit soul. This is confirmed within all religious scriptures of the world.

The third platform of consciousness is the transcendental level but this can only be experienced by those who lift themselves beyond the sensual and intellectual levels by austerity and penance toward the higher goal of spiritual self-realisation. In sanskrit this austerity is called "tapasya". It means beginning to control the outer senses in order to progress towards experience of the "inner spiritual self". The practice of mantra meditation directly leads toward the platform of transcendental consciousness. It needs the sincerity of desire and the ultimate good fortune of meeting a teacher "whose eyes have seen the truth". It is said that "only one whose eyes have seen the truth can impart it to others". Those fortunate enough to gain instruction from a bona-fide guru, a soul fully liberated from material consciousness, should have assured success on the spiritual path. Without the grace of God and Guru, none can alone remove the covering veil of "maya", or "that which is not". "Not all things are as they seem" is a phrase we understand to be true even involving the mundane intricacies of everyday life.

The vibrations which surround us and are associated with ourselves have the greatest effect upon our lives especially the character and consciousness we develop. The great saints, rishis and seers spread their vibrations to great distances from wherever they are and these vibrations are of the greatest value to everyone and on all levels. The negative vibrations of those engaged in nefarious activities or evil of all sorts also spreads, which is why association with those of higher quality and nature is so important. We become like those with whom we associate and absorb their "thought vibration". Thus be careful of the company you keep!

The power of thought is the driving force behind all accomplishment. One who has learned how to direct the thought processes and to fully concentrate can have success at all endeavours. This is why the vibrations of "positive thinking" will bring about the desired results. Then, when we add speech to the thought vibration, the strength becomes doubled and, with physical effort put into the accomplishment, the potency becomes doubled again. The basis must be always in having the "faith" to accomplish the desired results. Although we must also use our powers of reasoning in thought, this can give rise to doubt which then destroys the power of the thought before results can be achieved. Therefore firm faith and confidence must be there for success on any level, be it physical, mental, or spiritual.

IN PERFECT COEXISTENCE
THE HARMONY & RHYTHM OF LIFE

All living beings must live in harmony in order to have any happiness or sense of peace. That the world today is lacking this harmonious rhythm is warning in itself that there are great cataclysmic changes soon to come on our planet earth. One who can bring harmony into balance in all things can understand the meaning to life, one who cannot remains a fool despite any acquired material knowledge. Humans become attracted by two opposites in the search for harmony. One is the direction of godliness and spiritual life, the other towards material life in the form of matter. By moving further towards the material we lose sight and remembrance of the spiritual. It is only when we bring ourselves into harmony with the will of the Supreme that our own harmony is ultimately realised.

There is harmony in God's creation between land and water, the sun and the moon and between the stars and planets. They are all connected and moving in a universal harmony. There is a purpose and reason for all things moving and non-moving. Even the calamities of earth's past (as well as those to come in the future) regardless of how awful they may seem to us, are simply an adjustment to restore universal harmony. There are individual as well as collective karmas between us due to thoughts, words and deeds created in ignorance and these negativities destroy harmony, thereby necessitating nature's intervention. Were all people to adhere to God's laws, the laws of nature, there would always be universal harmony within the world.

There is universal harmony, which we have been speaking of, and there is an eternal harmony, known only once we are purified of material designations and situated on the plane of transcendence. There is also a harmony we must maintain individually between our own body and soul and one to be maintained between us as separate individuals. Most people today are completely unaware of the actual needs of the soul, but are engaged in an endless struggle to obtain flickering material happiness of the body. This is never fulfilled. The more a person struggles to become materially comfortable, the more dissatisfied he becomes. Not able to see beneath the dictates of the mind he thinks this dissatisfaction is due to some other unfulfilled material desire and thus it is an endless struggle of frustration upon frustration. One desire begets another and on and on. It is like pouring gasoline on a fire to put it out. Attempting to satisfy the sensual cravings of the physical body only increases the fire of material desire. Acting in this way there is never an end to it, nor ever satiation of further material (bodily) desire.

To have harmony between body and soul we human beings must strive to learn love. If we watch each thought we think, each word we say and each action we perform, striving to bring them to a higher level, then the ultimate outcome of this effort will be peace and wisdom. The eternal soul's desires are what are important, not the temporary illusory desires born of the body. To have harmony the bodily desires must be brought to subservience to those of the soul.

To have harmony between ourselves and others the blindness of false egoism must be removed. This is what makes us look at everything through the eyes of self-interest and judge everything in relation to ourselves. We become unable to see our own faults, much less do anything about them, and are then also unable to see the good qualities and merits of others. Until we can become free from the spell of illusion (maya) we can never have harmony and peace within ourselves or between each other.

It is possible to see gradations of harmony within man, birds, and beasts. The lions and tigers are always restless and welcome no outsiders to their homes, although they be of the same species. All other forest animals live in fear of them due to their severely passionate nature. Animals which live on herbs and grasses such as cows, sheep, or goats live in herds due to greater harmony between them. They do not harm one another, but are sympathetic toward one another. This makes them share harmony, but also makes them vulnerable to other wild animals. Birds have a great harmony in that many of them, even different species, can live together in one tree. Many insects such as the ants or bees, can also be seen living and working in harmony. Many tribal and aboriginal peoples of the world lived together in harmony and with an empathy for the world around them. The American aboriginals, known as the American Indians, are an example of a people who valued harmony with nature, rather than the modern values of accumulation and waste.

Then there is tone and rhythm. Just as in music rhythm and harmony can be learned, so it is with our own lives. We must learn to distinguish tones within words and thus their hidden meanings. How else to distinguish the truth from a lie, sarcasm from sincerity, admiration from flattery, modesty from humility, arrogance from pride, whether they are directly or indirectly expressed? The rhythm is the balance between speech and action. One must speak at the proper time, otherwise it is better to keep silent. We smile in rhythm and harmony when a person laughs, offer a sympathetic word in the face of another's grief and so on. In all arenas of life there is a certain harmony and rhythm at the heart of it all.

POETRY AND MUSIC

If we pay attention to the world around us we can hear the poetry and music of nature in everything. All living beings make some contribution to this musical harmony. The trees are moving their leaves and branches to the rhythm of the wind. The ocean is delivering its song with each crashing wave and the sounds of wind through the hills and valleys is a musical delight. The thunder resounding in answer to the flash of lightening and the balanced harmony of all things reveal the music of nature. Animals in the forest, lions, wolves, birds and so many others sing their own individual songs. This is the way in which they communicate.

As humans our breathing and heart keep the tone and beat. Children will appreciate music and dance before they have learned to speak. Actually children express themselves with musical tones before they have gained the ability to form words. When we speak we use different tones to get different points and/or emotions across to others. Ancient languages such as Sanskrit, Hebrew, Arabic, or Pali cannot be mastered simply by learning the words and pronunciation. It is also necessary to learn the proper tones and rhythms as the same word can mean different things according to the tone and/or rhythm used. I experienced how difficult it is for a native English speaker to master such languages when I first studied the Thai language (the root language is the ancient Pali) in Thailand many years ago and again in India when attempting to learn Sanskrit. Even in modern English and other European languages there exists some tonal varieties, different pitches, rhythm, accents and pauses or rests, just as does music. Music is what gives a language its definite expression. That is why it is difficult to speak a foreign language perfectly. The words are not so difficult to learn but the music is more difficult to master.

All the ancient spiritual messages were given in song; the Bhagavad-Gita, Song of Soloman, Psalms of David and the Gathas of Zoroaster. In ancient times knowledge such as philosophy and religion, the arts and sciences were all expressed as poetry. One finds that the Bible, Kabbala, Vedas, Puranas, Mahabharata, Ramayana, and so on are all written in verse. The only scripture written in prose, rather than poetry, is the Koran, but even here there is some poetry to be found. Even to this day do we not all love to hear poetry, rather than just spoken words?

Soldiers would sing on the road to do battle. Workers doing very hard physical labour have, in every culture, found singing in unison helpful to them in making the strenuous work more bearable. A mother sings to her little baby to calm or lull the child to sleep. The appreciation of music can be seen in us all from our very birth. Music has the greatest effect not only on our minds but on our subtle bodies and the soul. In all religions musical instruments and singing are of the utmost importance. Different spirits are attracted to different types of musical vibrations.

There are five aspects to music. One induces bodily motion, another stimulates the intellect, a third shows artistic beauty, another seems to go straight to the heart and, finally, there is that which is uplifting for the soul. It is this last aspect which allows us to see into dimensions other than the outer physical plane of existence.

In India music has been preserved just as it was discovered by the ancients. It is based upon principles of "Raga". It is unlimited, extremely uplifting and inspirational. There are five sources of raga; mathematical variety, mystical inspiration, the musician's imagination, natural differentiations to different indigenous peoples of India and poetic idealism. The last created a world of ragas, one called rag (male), another ragini (female) and others are termed putra (sons) or bharja (daughters-in-law). As raga is creative and positive it is considered the male theme. As ragini is responsive and of a finer quality it is called female. Putras are created from mingling of ragas and raginis and bharja is that which corresponds and responds to the putra. There are six ragas, thirty-six raginis (six to each raga), forty-eight putras and forty-eight bharjas. Together they constitute a family.

Every individual raga has a leading or key note (Mukhya), a principal note (Wadi), a subordinate note (Sumwadi) and an enemy or dissonant note (Anuwadi). Each raga is different and distinct from another and gives a concise understanding for its use. The ocean of ancient India's classical music is indeed very deep. Notes must be held solidly and for the greatest length of time possible through their different degrees to be properly effective. To break is considered to destroy its life. Different notes need different lengths of life according to their character and their purpose.

Music expresses emotion and feeling, the territory of the mind. Through music we may express anything without the use of words, if we are trained in the correct composition and have the natural affinity to do so. The highest, most natural music is produced by the voice, as no other instrument can compare with it. The flute best expresses the quality of heart's emotions for it is played with the life's breath.

Dancing has also always been considered a sacred art and means of serving God. In the Hebrew Torah we see David dancing before the Lord and, in India, the "Gaudiya Vaishnava" sampradaya (lineage) expresses worship of Lord Krishna through chanting and dancing before the Lord and His devotees. In so many religions we find singing and dancing most integral parts of the worship of God. Even the modern leader of Jewish mysticism, the "Baal-Shem-Tov" would dance and sing in ecstasy saying over and over "it's the name of the Lord, the name of the Lord". Dancing over the years has greatly degenerated, due to use only for exercise or personal pleasure, whereas it is meant to be an expression of love for the Divine.

"Mysticism" is but the secret of sound vibration. "Religion" is but the process for keeping harmony within life. "Metaphysics" is the knowledge of all vibration and "science" the analytical understanding of the atom. The arrangement of metaphysics and science in harmony is termed "art", the rhythm of form "poetry" and the rhythm of sound vibration "music". Therefore music is the king of all art forms and sciences and within it is contained the ultimate absolute truth.

The highest use of music is glorification of the Supreme Lord and this is the hidden secret of mantra. The only mantras which will have effect, even if not chanted perfectly in tone or rhythm, are those glorifying the unlimited names of God. All other mantras must be chanted perfectly in these respects in order to obtain the desired results. Now that I have given some prelude by discussing sound vibration, poetry and music, let me lead into the primary subject matter of this section, namely the mantra.

MANTRA...SACRED SOUND VIBRATION

Mantra meditation is often called "Mantra Yoga", considered to be a part of "Nada Yoga", which means the "yoga of sound". The word "yoga" means to "link with God" and this is the ultimate goal of all yoga. Today many people know nothing of yoga. Although used as a means to keeping good physical condition, in reality this is but a by-product of yoga. The physical postures or "asanas" are to help bring the senses under control in order to prepare for meditation. Control over the urges of the external senses (tongue, belly, and genitals) is required to actually engage in true meditation. Ultimately the mind will be also brought under control. Yoga is the science of self-realisation as enunciated in the Vedas, India's ancient holy scriptures, which are told to be descended from God Himself, not from man's comprehensions and expositions of relative truths. Therefore Veda means "truth", and the truths contained are as universal and equally applicable today just as they were many thousands of years ago.

In the Vedas there are said to be four ages or "yugas" in each dawning of new creation, made up of a total of some millions of years. In each yuga there was a recommended system of yoga in accordance with the mentality and ability of the populace during the time. At this time we are in the early stages of the "Kali-Yuga" (5,000 years have passed and 427,000 years remain), also known as the "age of quarrel and hypocrisy", a time when both our lives and memories are extremely short. Therefore in this age it is not possible for us to engage in the mystic yoga system. To practice this system there must be complete control of all senses, ultimately going into yogic trance as a prelude to self-realisation. (Oh yes, I almost forgot......it's necessary to spend some thousands of years doing so to achieve the goal by undergoing this difficult process!)

Therefore in this age it is not possible to achieve in this way as, not only do we live even less than 100 years, but who among us can concentrate with such intensity in silence, oblivious to all bodily urges or conveniences? Accordingly in this period mantra yoga, or mantra meditation, is the only viable means for self-realisation. There are many scriptural injunctions confirming that the "holy names of God" are the only means of crossing the ocean of maya (illusion) in order to become realised and thus free from the bonds of material life.

The great rishis, seers or saints of ancient India passed down these sacred sound vibrations for the benefit of all life but especially for human society, for only in the human form of life can one obtain spiritual realisation. Although animals benefit from hearing transcendental sound vibrations, they cannot achieve spiritual self-realisation unless or until they are promoted to the human form of life. These sacred sound vibrations are known to promote healing on all levels, whilst, at the same time, awakening the chakras within our ethereal, or subtle, bodies.

Mantras are always sung to a melody (raga), although it is generally monophonic, or individual, sounds which may "seem" to be without harmony. The Greeks, as did other cultures, understood music to be mathematical and, as Pythagoras taught, they made the equally interesting connection between sound, music and the science of astronomy. In "Poetica" Aristotle stated that poetry was comprised of language, rhythm and sound. He also pointed towards the potency of sound vibrations to influence human thoughts and emotions.

THE MEANING OF MANTRA

Mantras, being sacred sound vibrations, are composed of sacred syllables representative of and containing within great spiritual power, or energy. Utilising mantras allows us to concentrate and focus this spiritual energy. The mantras were perceived originally by the great seers or rishis from the primeval or cosmic ether and translated into very definite syllables with rhythm and melody.

The word "mantra" is composed, in sanskrit, of two root words. "Man" means "mind", or "thinking", and "tra" to "release or free". Therefore the meaning is to free the mind and thinking from the material sphere of consciousness and to be able to transcend the wheel of "samsara" or "birth and death within this physical world".

Chanting mantra promotes harmony on all levels as it awakens the spiritual self. Once awoken, ultimately the spiritual self, or soul, turns within to the source of all power and can direct spiritual energy not only for personal benefit but for the good of all others. All mantras have six aspects; a seer or rishi, a raga, a presiding deity (Devata), a seed sound (bija), power (shakti) and pillar (kilaka).

1 RISHIS Mantras have always come down from master to disciple, beginning with the ancient seers, or rishis. It is said that unless a mantra is received from an authorised source it will be ineffectual. Therefore this process has been kept intact since time immemorial. Just as different tones cause specific vibrations which have an effect on the physical and emotional self, practising mantra meditation correctly will allow the sound vibration to be connected with specific images and to understand that the sound vibration is contained within these images.

2 DEVATA Sound vibrations represent very definitive forms and repeated chanting of a mantra will gradually reveal the form of the deity, or devata, central to the mantra. This worship of the form then becomes the centre of the aspirant's consciousness. This allows the aspirant to develop a personal relationship with the presiding deity of the mantra.

There are many mantras for different results but the ultimate are the mantras for realising our relationship with the Supreme Lord. There are many levels of consciousness, as well as desire, among human beings and many mantras for achieving various goals. We will speak about the numerous types of mantras further on in this chapter but, suffice it to say, that the most important mantras are those which invoke the practitioner to bring about a desire for spiritual service, culminating in absolute love. At this point the aspirant may achieve the perfection of desire....to desire only that which is transcendental to this world of birth, death, old-age and disease.

3 BIJA Within each mantra is its seed (bija) which is its source of potency. Just as it is impossible to see the tree within the seed, yet it is there waiting for fructification, it is also not possible to see the spiritual self within until it is time. However, through regular discipline of chanting mantra the true "self" will eventually be realised. How quickly depends on the sincerity and desires of the aspirant. There are some mantras utilised simply for temporary gain within this material world and although I will give some descriptions of these, this is not the goal of chanting mantra. Only spiritual self-realisation is the ultimate goal. All other desires are stumbling blocks on the path to self-realisation.

4 PILLAR (KILAKA) is the will-power that an aspirant must gain to regularly practice the mantra until it becomes automatic.

5 SHAKTI is the power held within the mantra. Ultimately a taste develops, most especially in chanting mantras glorifying and extolling the qualities of God. We all have an "original" consciousness. The goal of life is to understand who we are, where we have come from and what is our purpose. Chanting mantras for any other purpose will not bear permanent fruit. Those utilised for any other purposes of a temporary nature must be chanted with perfect rhythm, tone and harmony and neither the raga, nor key, may be changed to any variation whatsoever. In today's world how many can develop such concentration and expertise over such a short life span?...not very many.

Fortunately, God is merciful and to indulge in the chanting of any ONE of the unlimited names of the Supreme Godhead as a devout mantra, even if imperfect, will have an effect. The only prerequisite is that the mantra is received from one who can properly impart it and train the aspirant in the basis of developing spiritual life and the resultant spiritual consciousness.

METHODS OF CHANTING MANTRA

1 KIRTAN is loud chanting congregationally so all who hear it may be benefited, even the lower living beings such as animals and plants. Kirtans are performed with drums and cymbals and in the case of Gaudiya Vaishnavism, the names of the Lord are chanted loudly while the participants dance in ecstasy. Anyone who has seen and heard the devotees of the Krishna Consciousness movement, or the "Hare Krishnas" chanting on the streets or in the temple has experienced a "kirtan".

It is considered the principal way of advancing on the path of "sadhana-bhakti", the process of bhakti-yoga. In the seventh canto of

Srimad-Bhagavatam it is stated, "Those who are intelligent in this age of Kali will worship the Lord through the performance of sankirtana". Sankirtan is kirtan done by a group of people, generally outdoors, where all within hearing distance may be benefited by hearing the chanting of the holy names. Elsewhere there are scriptural references such as in Bhakti-rasamrta-sindhu, Purva-vibhaga 2.145, "Kirtanam is defined as loudly giving voice to the glories of the Lord, beginning with the names, pastimes and qualities of Krishna".

2 BHAJAN Melodious chanting or singing of mantras accompanied by musical instruments. Generally stringed instruments and percussion are used although wind instruments may also be played. When a group of devotees (spiritual aspirants) comes together to sing transcendental songs based on mantras glorifying the Supreme, they are engaged in bhajan.

3 JAPA Repetition of a mantra is called "japa". Repeating the mantra aloud is called "vaikari japa", whispered softly it is termed "upamsu japa", repeating it within the mind is called "manasika japa" (again from the root Sanskrit word for mind "man"). Writing the mantra repetitively by hand is "likhita japa". All of these forms are beneficial and effective but most effective (especially in the beginning) is chanting loud enough to yourself so you can hear the chanting. This is called in Sanskrit "sravanam" (hearing) and "kirtanam" (chanting).

PURPOSE OF CHANTING

Chanting regularly with dedication and concentration will allow the development of devotion which will then bring the aspirant into harmony with the world around himself and the worlds within and without. It will bring peace and, if mantra is chanted with the sincere desire for self-realisation leading to God-realisation, then the aspirant will eventually come to a stage of bliss and ecstasy in transcendence. This may seem like fantasy for those who are fully imprisoned within the illusion of material sense gratification but for those who have risen above such animalistic sense perception it is a transcendent and eternal reality.

In Srimad-Bhagavatam 12.3.51 it is stated, "What was attained in

Satya-yuga through meditation, in Tretra-yuga through sacrifice and in Dvapara-yuga through Deity worship is realised in Kali-yuga through Hari-kirtana". (Hari is another name of God.) Remember that current lives last but a short span of time. Whatever gained in life materially is left behind at the time of death, or transmigration of the soul but whatever is gained on a spiritual level is never lost but carried forward to the next incarnation. In Bhagavad-Gita chapter 2, verse 40, this is confirmed thus, "In this endeavour there is no loss or diminution and a little advancement on this path can protect one from the most dangerous type of fear".

MANTRA PRACTICE

Practice of mantra in meditation acts as a magnet for spiritual energy and gradually the higher self, seen as having been dormant or asleep, is awakened. Only then can the soul understand what was enunciated by Sri Chaitanya Mahaprabhu in Bengal, India 500 years ago as "achintya bheda bheda tattva" or "simultaneous oneness with and difference from God". Mantras coming from an unbroken chain of spiritual masters in a disciplic succession (called a "parampara"), act to gradually purify the practitioner of contamination from eons of association with matter and link the disciple to the guru in a special relationship in which the teacher can impart wisdom to the aspiring disciple according to their ability.

In one Vedic scripture called "Mahajana-karika" it is said, "Transcendental knowledge, which is received through the system of 'parampara', beginning with Brahma, the creator and which is embodied in the Sruti is known as amnayaha, or the authorised sacred tradition".

Students must be astute to understand who is qualified to be guru. A verse from "Vayu-Purana" states the qualification as "An acarya is one who fully understands the conclusions of the revealed scriptures and whose behaviour reflects his deep realisation. He is a living example for he teaches the meaning of the scriptures both by word and deed".

In practice generally "japa-mala" or japa beads are used. They are a strand of beads carved from the sacred tulasi tree (always used by devotees of Lord Krishna or Vishnu), or other woods, or seeds such as the Rudraksha beads used in Shaivism. Other materials such as crystal, jewels, gold, or silver are also used but these are generally for mantras to gain material wealth. The strand contains 108 beads as 108 is a holy number. The 1 symbolises the Supreme energy, or Godhead. 0 symbolises completeness as God's creation is perfect and complete and the 8 symbolises eternity. (Mantras for material gain will use strands with fewer beads, for example a wealth mantra has 30 beads in the strand.)

At the top of the strand is a unique bead, carved differently from the rest, called the "Krishna bead" or "Mount Meru". This bead is not fingered during chanting. Beginning from the first bead the bead is gently rolled between the thumb and middle finger while the mantra is being repeated. One repetition on each bead is chanted until reaching the "Krishna bead". This bead is not rolled between the fingers as the rest but when reaching it the process is to then go back in the opposite direction. One completion of 108 mantras (the number of beads on the strand) constitutes one "round" of mantra, or a round of "japa".

Different devotees make different vows, according to the instructions of their guru, as to the number of rounds of mantra completed daily. Using beads helps the concentration and also helps to dissipate nervous energy. These beads become infused with spiritual energy coming from within the devotee and should be considered sacred, to be kept in a special place and never to be left on the ground.

It is best to find a quiet time and place to chant. Better to chant attentively for 5 minutes, fully concentrating on the mantra, than to chant for an hour when the mind and senses are too disturbed by unnecessary stimuli. Bathe, then create a spiritually conducive atmosphere by lighting incense and doing some deep breathing to relax the mind and body. If chanting mantras for spiritual liberation, sit facing the north and if the mantras are for fulfilment of material desires, sit facing the east.

Sit down cross-legged, if possible, but if this is difficult simply find a comfortable position that can be maintained for at least a short while. Its no good getting into a "lotus pose" if your mind is screaming from the physical discomfort. However, if this pose is comfortable, there is no better position for meditation.

Hold the beads at the level of the heart chakra, which represents devotion and the desire to transcend the "lower" self. Generally the beads are kept "hidden" by keeping them in a specially made "bead bag" which has a hole to put your hand and a convenient smaller hole opposite the hand hole where the forefinger can stick out. This makes it easier to chant using the thumb and middle finger. Then try to relax and forget about all daily mundane thoughts or activities for a while. Begin to repeat the mantra while rolling each individual bead between your thumb and middle (third) finger. Breathe deeply and regularly and allow the mantra to wash over your mind. Allow it to enter the earholes by careful listening and to dance on your tongue by the attentive chanting.

After some time you will feel often a great release of pent-up emotions and feeling. There may be tears, there may be so many thoughts of wasted time in this life (and maybe other lives). Just keep bringing yourself back by concentrating on hearing and chanting. If you begin to fall asleep, then assume another position or stop your chanting for the time being. Remember that regular practice is necessary and it will take a little time to begin to realise the benefits on the spiritual, emotional and even physical levels. Anything worth attaining is worth the patience and fortitude. If you want something cheap there are any number of charlatans waiting to cheat you with so-called spiritual processes to "make you God". God never "becomes God". He is eternally the Supreme Godhead. We, as individual souls (atma), are part and parcel of God endowed with all qualities of God but not in the same quantity, just as drops of water from the ocean are no different in content than the entire ocean, other than their quantity. If you really want truth and self-realisation and ultimately God-realisation you must develop patience and humility. There's no short cut or "new-age" way of minimising the process you undergo in the search for spiritual liberation. On the contrary this very "old-age" process of mantra meditation will infuse you with spiritual energy and remembrance of knowledge gained and forgotten over the millennia of time.

When an aspiring disciple has attained firm faith, and the spiritual master feels the disciple ready, he may offer "diksha", or spiritual initiation. It is of utmost importance to find a realised teacher eventually in order to make real spiritual advancement. In the "Narada Pancaratra, Bharadvaja-samhita 2.34" the following is written, "When the guru gives the mantra to his disciple according to the rules and regulations of pancaratrika-viddhi, then, by the influence of that mantra, the disciple never takes birth again. A humble disciple conducts himself with great respect for his spiritual master as if he is a son of the guru. To such a humble disciple, who has been purified by the appropriate samskaras (rituals), the guru teaches the meaning of the mantra. This is the way that spiritual initiation is performed according to the rules and regulations of scripture". Therefore we also see from this verse that the first important quality of a sincere disciple is humility. Without humility it is not possible to rise above the false ego of "I" and "mine", or to speak of engaging in spiritual practice under a bona-fide teacher.

From this verse we can understand that only one who can save his disciple from repeated birth and death in the material planetary systems should become a spiritual master, or guru.

BIJA (SEED) MANTRAS

As stated earlier, as seeds hold within them the fruit of a full-grown tree, similarly bija, or seed, mantras hold within them shakti (spiritual potency or energy). There are different seed mantras, each with their own shakti. It is told in the Vedas that the first primordial sound produced at the time of creation of the universes was the "OM" mantra. It is the original sound.

In Bhagavad-Gita, Chapter 10 verse 25, Krishna says, "of vibrations I am the transcendental Om", also in chapter 7 verse 8 "I am....the syllable Om in the vedic mantras". Again in chapter 17 verse 24, "Thus the transcendentalists undertake sacrifices, charities and penances, beginning always with Om, to attain the Supreme". This most important seed mantra is almost always found to be preceding the words used in various mantras.

There are other seed mantras which are used and especially by young children as they can easily repeat them with enthusiasm, being as short as one or two syllables. Some examples are as follows:-

1	**KSHASRAUM**	This is the bija of Narasimha (half-man / half-lion incarnation of Vishnu). It makes you fearless and happy.
2	**SHRI**	This is Lakshmi bija, for material prosperity.
3	**Kalim**	This is the Kamraj bija which is said to fulfil desires.
4	**Aim**	This is Saraswati bija, to become learned in all forms of knowledge.
5	**Dum**	This is Durga bija, again for fulfilling material desires.
6	**Harim**	This is Bhuvaneshvari bija, also called Maya bija, for becoming a leader and fulfilling desires for power.
7	**Krim**	This is Kali bija, for destruction of your enemy.
8	**Gam Glaum**	This is Ganesha bija, for removing obstacles and gaining success in all endeavours.
9	**Lam**	This is Pritvi bija (mother earth) for raising productive agricultural products.
10	**Yam**	This is Vayu bija (demigod of wind) for bringing sufficient rain.
11	**AAM**	This is Brahma bija
12	**UM**	This is Vishnu bija
13	**RAM**	This is Rudra bija

CATEGORIES OF MANTRAS AND YANTRAS

1	**SHANTIKARAN**	These mantras are for curing disease and are also given by astrologers for warding off evil planetary influences (see planetary section).

2	**VASHIKARAN**	These mantras are for bringing people under control or influence.
3	**STAMBHAN**	These mantras are for thwarting an enemy's actions.
4	**VIDESHAN**	These mantras are for creating problems between several or a group of people.
5	**UCCHATAN**	These mantras are for distracting enemies or others to keep them away from their homes.
6	**MARAN**	These mantras are for causing death of a person or people regardless of where they are.
7	**MOKSHA**	These mantras are for liberation from repeated birth and death within this material world.

INDIVIDUAL MANTRAS

1 MAHA-MANTRA   *"Hare Krishna Hare Krishna Krishna Krishna Hare Hare Hare Rama Hare Rama Rama Rama Hare Hare"*

This mantra is called "maha", the greatest mantra. It is the most powerful chanted mantra. If you only learn and regularly chant this 16 word mantra, it is sufficient for awakening the higher self to it's true nature as spirit and will allow you to make spiritual advancement to the point of full self-realisation. It is calling for the energy and mercy of the Supreme Personality of Godhead and there are no hard and fast rules for the chanting of this Supreme mantra.

In the "Ananta-Samhita" within the Vedas we find the following:-"This sixteen name, thirty-two syllable mantra is the maha-mantra in the age of Kali by which all living beings can be delivered. One should never abandon chanting this maha-mantra and take to other so-called purificatory processes which are practiced by rascals, or engage in chanting other metrical compositions of the name of Krishna that are against the pure conclusions of the scriptures, or are filled with rasabhasa (scripturally unfounded conclusions or practice). About this divinely spiritual maha-mantra, which delivers one from material existence, the original guru, Lord Brahma, has said, 'kali-santaranadi srutite', ('the srutis section of the Vedas have declared this mantra to be the best means of deliverance in the age of Kali'). Having all heard this from Brahma, the sons and disciples of Brahma, beginning with Narada, all accepted the Hare Krishna maha-mantra and having once meditated on it attained perfection".

In the "Kalisantarana Upanishad" it is stated, "The sixteen names of the Hare Krishna mantra destroy all the inauspiciousness of the age of Kali. This is the conclusion of all the Vedas. Also in the "Agni-Purana" it is written, "Whoever chants this mantra, even neglectfully, will attain the supreme goal of life. Of this there is no doubt". So you can see this is the most important mantra to learn!

2 GAYATRI MANTRA   *"Om bhur bhuva swa tatsa vetur varenyam bhargo devasya dhimahi dhiyo yona prachodayat"*

This is actually only the first line of the full gayatri mantra which is chanted morning, noon and night by brahmins (priests) offering respects to the Supreme. It is only for advanced spiritual aspirants. Gayatri mantra is said to achieve liberation. A verse supporting this conclusion (yet also supporting the conclusion that only the maha-mantra is a necessity in this present age) from the "Chaitanya Charitamrita, Adi-Lila 7.73" states, "Through the gayatri mantra one attains liberation from material existence. Through the holy name one attains the lotus feet of Krishna".

3 SHIVA MANTRA   *"Om Namah Shivaye"*

This mantra is to fulfil all desires and to lead to moksha (spiritual liberation). There are no restrictions in chanting it, and it is used by devotees of Lord Shiva.

4 NARAYANA MANTRA *"Om Namo Narayanaye Namaha"*

This mantra is extremely powerful for spiritual advancement and is calling on Lord Narayana (an expansion of Vishnu). There are no restrictions in the chanting of this or any other mantra of the "Vishnu Sahastranam" (the thousand names of Vishnu).

5 VASUDEV MANTRA *"Om Namo Bhagavate Vasudevaye"*

This mantra is offering great respects to the "literary incarnation" of Vishnu, Vasudev, who has written down the vedic knowledge for the benefit of human society. It is a powerful and uplifting mantra and can be used without limitations.

6 GANAPATI (GANESHA) MANTRA

> *"Om Sharem Harim Klim Glaum Gam Ganapataye Namaha"*

This mantra is always chanted first in all vedic sacrifices to remove any and all obstacles in the way. Lord Ganesha (Ganapati) is the remover of obstacles, and also the giver of success in endeavours.

A shorter version is *"Om Gam Ganapataye Namaha"*

7 HANUMAN MANTRA *"Om Hoom Hanumate Rudratamakaye Hoom Phut Swaha"*

This mantra is to Lord Hanuman, the "monkey god", who is the greatest devotee of Lord Rama. The story of His exploits are famous from the epic "Ramayana" (also known as the "Ramakyen" in Thailand) He is said to give good qualities of character.

8 SARASWATI MANTRA *"Om Aim Kling Saum Saraswatiye Namaha"*

This mantra is one of those known as "Devi mantras" (for Saraswati, Kali, Durga, Tripura Bala, and Lakshmi). This mantra will give a great education.

SHANTI MANTRAS

There are many mantras used for specific diseases or ailments such as the **"ARUNA MANTRA"** for eye disease *"Om Arun Haem Phut Swaha"*,

This mantra must be repeated 10,000 times. Then water is purified by chanting the mantra 7 times and the water used to wash the eye.

For Health:

> *"Om Aaham Veshvanye Bhootva Praneenam*
> *Dahmakshiet Pranapam Samyukta Pchamyananm*
> *Chaturvidham"*

This mantra is chanted 3 times over some water to infuse it with potency, which is then drunk.

Preventing Miscarriage during Pregnancy:

> *"Pumansam Patram Jancy Tam Pumananu Jayatam*
> *Bhavati Putranam Mata Jatanam Jamyashyam Yan"*

This mantra from the Atharva Veda (3.23) should be chanted in the morning with a vessel of water during morning puja (worship). While reciting the mantra sprinkle a little water on the woman, then give her some to drink.

Mantras For Birth of a Child to Childless Couple:

1   *"Om Sri Haring Kaling Galeen"*
       "Om Devekisut Govind Vasudev Jagatpite"
       "Dehi ye Tancy Krishna Tawamahem Sharanam
       Gata"

Chant this mantra 30,000 times.

2   *"Om Namo Bhagavate Jagatprasutaye Nam"*

Chant also 30,000 times.

3   *"Om Kaling Gopalveshdhraya Vasudevaye Hoong Phut Swaha"*

Chant 10,000 times after performing puja to Lord Krishna.

For Birth of a Son:

"Om Haring Haring Haroong Putram Kuru Kuru Swaha"

This mantra is to be chanted before Lord Shiva and Parvati 108 times a day for 21 days.

For intelligence, education and wealth:

"Om Kring Kring Kring"

This must be chanted 1008 times.

PUJA, YOGA, & THE PATH OF ENLIGHTENMENT

Puja, or worship, is a part of a spiritual aspirant's daily activity aimed at bringing one closer to self-realisation and God-consciousness by performing service for your worshipped deity, the form of God to which one has greatest attraction. The demigods who live in the higher planetary systems are also worshipped by those who desire material benefits, such as wealth or promotion to heavenly planets after the present birth. In Bhagavad-Gita chapter 17, verse 3, it is said, "According to one's existence under the various modes of nature, one evolves a particular type of faith. The living being is said to be of a particular faith according to the modes he has acquired". If you actually desire liberation from the miseries of repeated birth, disease, old-age and death then you must become self-realised. By understanding the difference between spirit and matter you can then understand that true nature is spirit and that the body (made of material elements) is temporary. Why go on making plans to provide comfort for a body that will soon be finished?

The process of puja can be as simple as prayer and making basic offerings of leaves, flowers and water, or as opulent as your means provides. It must come from the heart. God, as Supersoul, dwells within the heart of every living entity and knows all our desires and activities. Having been through countless births and deaths of innumerable material bodies since time immemorial we go through one illusion after another, thinking we are the body.....right up until the time of death when we must leave it. What makes human life different from animal life is religious devotion and the ability to reflect and rationalise. Otherwise we are eating, sleeping, mating and defending what we mistakenly think are our own possessions just as the animals do. Think about it! What makes our eating, sleeping, sex-lives and protection of our "territory" any different from a dog's or cat's? They also eat, sleep, have sex and fear intrusion upon what is "theirs"......and then die, leaving the body for another one.

It is of the utmost importance that we not misuse this valuable opportunity afforded to us in human form to begin to become self-realised, otherwise there are no guarantees as to the next birth. In Bhagavad-Gita Ch.8 verse 6 Krishna states to Arjuna, "Whatever state of being one remembers when he quits his body, that state he will attain without fail". Therefore it is our consciousness that determines what our next birth will be.

The Vedas tell us that there are 8,400,000 different species of life within this material world throughout the various planetary systems. Human life is meant for gaining spiritual knowledge. Otherwise we run the risk of sometimes degrading ourselves to less than progressive births as humans or even lower life forms. The "karma-khanda" sections of the Vedas describe "dharma" (duties) people must perform in this life to have all necessities provided in this life and promotion to a better life in the future. Even so such advancement is temporary; as when you have exhausted the results of pious actions by enjoying life in the heavenly planets with superior facility for sense gratification (if one has acted in such a way as to be promoted to such a life), for millions of years by our calculations, you return to the earthly stratosphere again.

In Bhagavad-Gita Krishna says, "Men of small intelligence worship the demigods and their fruits are limited and temporary. Those who worship the demigods go to the planets of the demigods, but My devotees ultimately reach My supreme planet". Similarly if one is extremely sinful in this life one may be "demoted" to hellish planetary systems where the suffering experienced is far worse than anything we can imagine here.

Therefore "real" religion means understanding and performing "Sanatana dharma" (our eternal duties). Once one can understand that they are indeed spirit soul and not the material body, then the realisation dawns that I am not Howard, or Bill, or Susan, or Rajiv, or Michiko. That is simply the name we are called in this life. In the last life you were someone else and you related to that name, the family and associates around you and maintained attachments to them and the world you lived in. At the time of death all is finished. Then in the next life it begins all over again, this time in a new body, with a new name, and a new situation that we then mistakenly think is ours. We are simply "chewing the chewed", or going through the same bewildering circumstances again and again. We must understand what our eternal duties to God and to our "real selves" are and how we can once more regain our original form and consciousness. In Srimad-Bhagavatam 1.2.9 it is said, "All dharmas are certainly meant for ultimate liberation". Only then will there be real satisfaction and happiness and only then can we transcend this world of birth and death for eternal life in the spiritual stratosphere. Confirmed in Bhagavad-Gita Ch.8 verse 16 with Krishna stating to Arjuna, "From the highest planet in the material world down to the lowest, all are places of misery wherein repeated birth and death take place. But one who attains to My abode, O son of Kunti, never takes birth again".

Mantras are not magical incantations, but words of "power" which can help one to gain temporary material benefits, if that is one's level of consciousness, or to gain permanent spirtual benefit, that does not end with the death of the body. In any case sincerity of heart and worship of the presiding "deity" is necessary. It will not be possible to gain the desired results unless one performs some worship along with the mantra; all combined this has the desired effects if we have the steadfastness to do so.

So, what if we begin our spiritual practice, but due to previous bad habits and conditioning we fall back into material activities? Is it possible to just forget all one has learned? Well, in Bhagavad-Gita Ch.6 verse 40 we read, "The Blessed Lord said: Son of Pritha, a transcendentalist engaged in auspicious activities does not meet with destruction either in this world or in the spiritual world; one who does good, My friend, is never overcome by evil".

What if we practice yoga and mantra meditation, but cannot complete our mission or fully attain the goal due to being diverted by material desires? Bhagavad-Gita Ch.6 verse 41 states, "The unsuccessful yogi, after many, many years of enjoyment on the planets of the pious living entities, is born into a family of righteous people, or into a family of rich aristocracy", and verse 42, "Or he takes his birth in a family of transcendentalists who are surely great in wisdom. Verily, such a birth is rare in this world".

The conclusion is that it's always better to attempt to raise one's consciousness through mantra and spiritual practice, even if in this birth it's impossible to perfect. Material life, of looking always for sense pleasure, is chasing after a whim in which satisfaction is never found. Better to be a yogi, for regardless of how long it takes, eventual success is assured.

Yoga means to "link with God". Today it is most often proposed as a means of keeping a healthy body, but in reality this is a side-effect. Yoga is for spiritual development. In Bhagavad-Gita reference is made to the "Patanjali Yoga System" in Ch. 4 verse 27, "Those who are interested in self-realisation, in terms of mind and sense control, offer the functions of all the senses, as well as the vital force (breath), as oblations into the fire of the controlled mind". Within the "Yoga-Sutra" of Pantanjai technical information is given on the process of controlling the 10 types of airs within the body. The goal is to purify the soul from material attachment. When one engages in using the material senses for external gratification, the soul is called "parag-atma" (atma is the soul). The goal of yoga is to withdraw from material activities using the airs of the body to seek self-realisation. At that time the soul is called "pratyag-atma". Ultimately we must seek service unto the supreme Godhead to satisfy the craving of the soul. In Srimad-Bhagavatam 1.6.35 we find this relevant verse, "By yoga practice one may be able to control the senses and become relatively free from lust and greed, but this will never satisfy the soul. Only devotional service to Krishna gives complete satisfaction to the soul".

The eightfold yoga system which instructs how to control the external senses, eventually bringing the mind under complete control, is very difficult for us to perform in this age. From Bhagavad-Gita's description in the 6th chapter, verses 13-14 we can see why; "One should hold one's body, neck, and head erect in a straight line and stare steadily at the tip of the nose. Thus, with an unagitated, subdued mind, devoid of fear, completely free from sex life, one should meditate upon Me (Krishna/God) within the heart and make Me the ultimate goal of life".

The system of raising the life air (kundalini) from the chakra at the base of the spine to the succeeding chakras at the lower abdomen, the navel, the heart, the throat, between the eyebrows and finally to the crown chakra at the top of the head, is all but impossible to perform in this day and age. Ideally a person must be completely celibate to even begin the process and very few people can even contemplate this state of being. In other ages it was possible to become self-realised by this process, ultimately coming face-to-face with "Paramatma" (Supersoul, the expansion of God in the hearts of all). The culmination was to push the life airs through the crown chakra (at an auspicious time determined by astronomical calculation), burning the body up in yogic fire and transferring the life force to the desired goal either in a higher planetary system or merging with the Brahmajyoti (the effulgent "white light"). This was through meditating on impersonal features of God.

Meditating on the personal features of God by the yogis would allow them to achieve the spiritual planets (Vaikuntha-lokas), from where having gone, one never returns to the misery of repeated birth and death within the material world. In Bhagavad-Gita Ch.8 verse 13 it is said, "After being situated in this yoga practice and vibrating the sacred syllable Om, the supreme combination of letters, if one thinks of the Supreme Personality of Godhead and quits his body, he will certainly reach the spiritual planets".

In this age of "Kali", a time of short memory, little ability for difficult austerities and short life-span, it is next to impossible to perform such a process to achieve the desired goal. Therefore in this age the only viable means to self-realisation is mantra meditation, using mantras composed of the holy names of God. The "sankirtan-yajna", or the congregational chanting of these names is said to be the only "yajna" (spiritual austerity) necessary for humans to perform in this age. This is stated in Srimad-Bhagavatam (11.5.29), "In this age of Kali, people who are endowed with sufficient intelligence will worship the Lord, who is accompanied by His associates, by performance of sankirtana-yajna". Also in the Brihan-Naradiya Purana it is stated, "In this age of quarrel and hypocrisy the only means of deliverance is chanting the holy name of the Lord. There is no other way. There is no other way. There is no other way".

Therefore if one truly desires "enlightenment" it's necessary to first become enlightened as to one's actual nature as spirit soul, and to then understand what is our "eternal duty" (sanatana-dharma). Then it behooves us to begin the path to enlightenment using a bona-fide process of self-realisation, which in this age is mantra meditation and spiritual service to God known as Bhakti-Yoga. Bhakti means love and Bhakti-yoga is the attainment of love of God. But before one can attain such a lofty goal, first must be developed love for ourselves and all others. To do so one must first raise oneself to the platform of goodness (sattva) by consciously developing the godly qualities of honesty, cleanliness, mercy, compassion, kindness, equanimity, and so on.

By using mantra under the tutelage of a learned soul, gradually becoming detached from materialism and developing higher human qualities, anyone can begin to liberate themselves from the wheel of "samsara" (repeated birth and death in the material planetary systems), find inner peace and joy in the present, and guarantee unending spiritual bliss in the future.

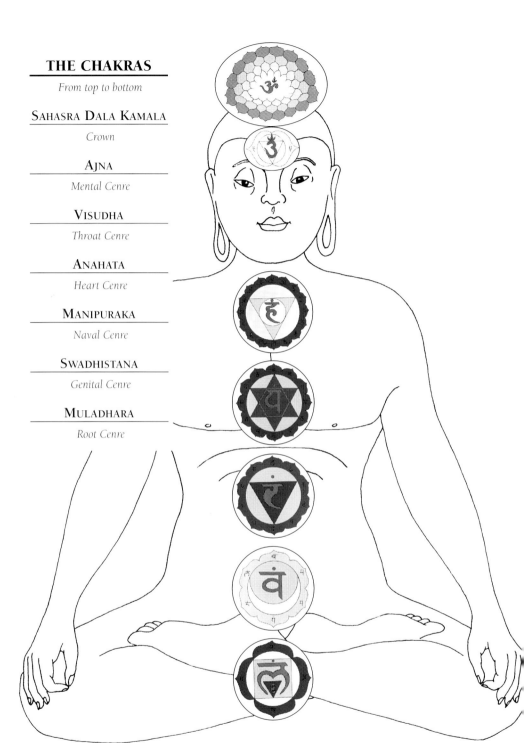

THE CHAKRAS

From top to bottom

SAHASRA DALA KAMALA

Crown

AJNA

Mental Cenre

VISUDHA

Throat Cenre

ANAHATA

Heart Cenre

MANIPURAKA

Naval Cenre

SWADHISTANA

Genital Cenre

MULADHARA

Root Cenre

THE CHAKRAS

The seven chakras, or "lotuses", are the centres of consciousness situated within our subtle, or astral, bodies. The object of the yogis and tantrics is to ultimately, through much long, arduous practice, bring the life air of "kundalini shakti" up the spinal column and through the chakras, one after another, until finally reaching the crown chakra. These chakras are the centres of sushumna and I will describe their positions, attributes, and representations.

MULADHARA CHAKRA

This chakra is situated at the base of the spine, in between the anus and the external genitalia. This lotus is of a blood-red colour and upon it's four petals are the four sanskrit letters "vam", "sam", "sham" and "saem". They are in different tones and hues of golden colour. In the centre is a square shape, representing the earth. It is a yellow colour. Upon this square is the elephant "Iravatham", bearing the sanskrit letter "lam". In the centre is either four-armed Ganesh or, in some, Brahma with four heads. Either is the presiding deity of this chakra.

Central to this lotus is the "Dhakini Shakti". In the centre is a triangle carrying "Kama bhija" or "Klim". Above this is a "Siva lingam" of black colour and, above the lingam, the kundalini in three coils. To open or arouse this chakra is the goal of "Raj Yoga" and, once awakened, an aspirant becomes free, or absolved of the reactions to any previous sinful activity.

SWADHISTANA CHAKRA

This chakra is situated at the root of the sexual organs, just below the navel. This lotus is of a very deep vermilion colour. Upon it's petals are six sanskrit letters with "bija" letters "Bam", "Mam", "Yam", "Ram" and "Lam".

Centrally located is the white "Varuna Mandala", or the region of water, in a half-moon crescent shape. Seen gliding upon the water is a makra (alligator) with the bija letter "Vam". Riding upon the alligator is Lord Vishnu holding conch shell, lotus flower, sudarshana chakra (disc) and mace (club) in His four hands. In the very centre is "Rakini-Shakti", a fearful-looking deity with four arms and three eyes.

MANIPURAKA CHAKRA

This chakra is found above the navel, just below the solar plexus and is of a violet colour. This lotus possesses ten petals which has upon it the bija letter representative of the "Agni-Mandala", or the region of fire.

Central to it is the bija letter "Ram" situated upon a goat and upon the bija is found Rudra (a form of Lord Shiva) riding upon a bull. Directly in the centre is "Lakini Shakti" with three eyes, three faces and four arms.

ANAHATA CHAKRA

This chakra is found in the vicinity of the heart, so is often referred to as the "heart chakra". This is the seat of the soul or "Jivatma", as well as the form of God, "Ksirodakshayi Vishnu," in the heart of all living beings called "Paramatma" or "Supersoul". There is a core in the centre of a red colour, surrounded by ten petals of the lotus which are of a golden-pink colour. The bija letters are the "Vayu-Mandala", (air), arranged in a hexagonal shape and of a smoky colour.

Centrally located is an inverted triangle beaming with light. Upon it is the "Vayu Bija" riding upon a black deer. Also present is the presiding deity of "Ishwara" who has two arms, but three eyes. Directly over this centre is a deity of the name "Kakini", who is dressed in yellow garments and sits upon a red flower. This deity gives the boon of fearlessness. Within the triangle is a "bana lingam", and directly below is a lotus of eight petals upon which the "Jivatma" moves. It says within the tantra that, through meditation with very great concentration upon this lotus, there will be heard ten sounds. These sounds are said to have excellent healing effects.

VISUDHA CHAKRA

This chakra is found at the base of the throat. The lotus has sixteen petals of a greyish colour. The letters upon it are of a red colour and centrally located is a circular white space representative of the sky or "Akash Mandala". A triangle is in the middle section upon which is the "Chandra Mandala", the region of the Moon. Upon this mandala is the "Akasha Bija" sitting upon a white elephant. Within the bindu is "Sada Shiva" who wears the tiger skin and has five faces, three eyes and ten arms holding different weapons. He is riding a bull.

Centrally located within the Chandra Mandala is a deity called "Sakini" who has five faces, three eyes and four hands. It is said that one having the vision of this lotus will be free from disease of any kind.

Ajna Chakra

This chakra is of the name "Trikuti" and is positioned between the two eyebrows. It is made up of two petals of a white colour upon which are two bija letters. Directly in the centre resides the deity of the name "Hakini Shakti", who has six faces of white colour, three arms and three eyes. There is a triangle with bija, "Rudra Granthi" and the "Hita Longa" which is white and gives off sparks of fire similar to bolts of lightening. According to the teachings of mystic yoga these sparks of fire radiate to the "Brahmarandra" or the centre of the "higher self".

On beyond this point is the "Sahasrara Kamal" (thousand-petalled lotus), where is situated the "third eye". It is said that those able to bring all force and concentration to this area are able to burn all past karmas and achieve "mukti", or liberation from birth and death within this material world.

Sahasra Dala Kamala

This chakra is at the top of the head at the "cranial hole", that part of the skull which is still open when a child is born. Upon its thousand petals are fifty letters, which are repeated twenty times over. Once an adept has brought the kundalini through the six chakras to enter within the Sahasra or "Sat Chakra", a superconscious state is achieved known as "samadhi". This is the state of consciousness which is completely concentrated upon the lotus feet of the Supreme Lord. In the "Mayavada" school it is considered to be the merging of individual consciousness with the infinite consciousness, or the union between Shakti and Shiva in the Shaivite school of thought. The sat chakra is said within the scripture "Gandharva Malika Tantra" to contain the divine all desire-fulfilling tree (Kalpa-Vriksha) and that again any seeing this lotus is freed from the cycle of samsara (birth and death).

YANTRAS

Often when I bring up the subject of "yantra" in the west, I get blank stares of incomprehension. If I then say "sacred geometry" some will understand, as this is what the modern scholars of ancient Egypt refer to their ancient system of yantra as. Many will also understand if I mention "mandala" as the Tibetan forms of mandala are more well known in the west. The particular shapes and figures have often been picked up and used commercially as poster prints which people place on their walls for decoration, not having the slightest idea of the intent of such a diagram. Many ancient Vedic yantras, which are the oldest known, such as the concentric expanding diagram of "Sri Yantra" are mistakenly referred to as "mandalas" by the so-called "new-age" community.

All ancient cultures had sacred geometric designs representative of their Gods, which had a mantra (or sacred sound vibration) that corresponded to it. The Indians, Egyptians, Jews, Chinese, and Mayans all had systems of "planetary yantras" used to combat malefic influences. Yantra is the ultimate "symbology". In the Vedic culture we find much power and energy said to be held within sacred geometric symbols. They are to be found throughout sacred scriptures, carved in stone, hidden within paintings and in temples.

One example of how a western "madman" tried to use these powers for personal gain (of an evil disposition) is the case of Adolph Hitler. The swastika is actually an ancient, holy symbol found in temples all over the east. It is especially seen in paintings and carved into the temples and thrones for deities of Lord Ganesh (the elephant-headed god of prosperity said to remove impediments and obstacles from the path of human endeavour). Hitler actually drew the symbol improperly and, although it looks like the original to the untrained eye at a glance, it is wrong and had no potency.

Furthermore there is much more to yielding the power behind yantra than simply having the diagram. As I've tried to show in the previous parts of this book, there is the dedication and effort required to yield the beneficial effects of chanting mantras, especially if they are for some material purpose. Yantras are not "lucky charms" to be worn or displayed as icons of power in and of themselves. Much specific knowledge and ability must go into their preparation and much dedication and worship is required to achieve the desired effects.

Yantra means a "mystical diagram", "talisman", or "instrument" which, if prepared and created by a qualified "Tantric" (one qualified in the knowledge and practice of Tantra) as well as utilised under their specific instructions for fruitful results, will help to gain the object or objects of desire or ambition. Yantras are used in worship (puja) and can also be an effective instrument used towards the aim of self-realisation. The Vedic scriptures speak of them as worshipable and they were used by the ancient saints, seers, and rishis.

Yantras and mantras are connected together as for each yantra (diagram) there is a corresponding mantra that must be used with it. They are representative of different deities from different demigods all the way up to the Supreme Personality of Godhead, Lord Krishna, or Lord Vishnu. There is also a definite relationship between them and the material elements of earth, water, fire, air and ether. By proper prayers, worship, and perfect recitation of specific mantras the material elements, or material nature, may be induced to move in a way the practitioner desires. This is not magic, nor trickery, but a highly evolved and developed science for exercising some control in this regard.

The different planets in our solar system have different effects on our daily lives here on earth and there are yantras for each planet which, when properly installed and worshipped, allow the aspirant to ward off certain malefic effects. This is the reason why a qualified vedic astrologer recommends mantras, yantras, or gemstones as a remedial measure to their clients. Properly utilised they are capable of making an inauspicious planetary influence less troublesome, or to negate the effect altogether. Besides countering negative effects we also desire to increase the planets' beneficial aspects in our lives by the use of these ancient tools.

A zero ("nought" to the British or "bindu" in Sanskrit) is the basis of the geometry through which the triangle is developed. It is said to represent the different desires within the heart, the ways of fulfilling them and the acquisition of knowledge.

This "bindu" is the central point. By concentrating on the bindu the ability to concentrate and build up a powerful mental or psychic force field is increased. It is broadened and, in it's expansion, many other kinds of shapes are formed. These figures or geometric shapes are what are termed the "yantra".

Although it would not be a difficult task for most of us to copy the form of a yantra, it would not have the desired effect. Furthermore to be perfectly honest, it would be all but useless if not created by a qualified person ("Tantric") and then "infused" with the specific energy via the medium of mantra. Otherwise it becomes just an interesting form or picture to look at, but has no real effect on time or circumstances within life.

The physical manifestation of the yantra itself is generally drawn or etched into metal, be it gold, silver, bronze, copper, lead, or stainless steel, although paper is sometimes used for their inscription. Such materials are long-lasting with the idea that when the worship, or puja, is performed, the person the yantra is meant for will have protection from evil and undesirable forces of nature. To constantly increase its effectiveness the user must perform certain worship and regularly chant the prescribed mantras. As explained in the section on mantras, sincerity of heart is a basic principle necessary for the results to be realised.

As a vedic astrologer I regularly recommend the use of remedial measures, although I have found that for most westerners the path of mantra and yantra is much more difficult to realise beneficial results through (materially speaking) than is the science of gemstone therapy. By obtaining a proper natural gemstone correctly set and installed with specific mantras, it will on its own act to ward off malefic (negative) planetary influences and attract benefic (positive) ones. Although always helpful, it is not necessary to continually perform worship of the gem (except initially) or chant the mantras after the initial installation, yet it will still have a constant protective influence. Mantras and yantras must be used with the utmost care, dedication and spiritual energy through regular puja and chanting to be effective.

Due to the highly advanced and evolved souls necessary to create, dedicate, install and worship the yantra initially, they may seem to be ineffective in this day and age. However, it is not due to any defects within the revealed knowledge and science of yantra, but to the lack of dedication and ability of most to achieve the results. These sacred diagrams of "yantra" are representative of time and space and can most especially be seen within the most sacred and powerful yantra, the "Sri Yantra". There are so many very exacting levels to be gone through in their preparation and specific rituals that absolutely must be performed perfectly during this step-by-step procedure, that their creation is extremely difficult and specialised.

There is an irrevocable connection between the yogic and tantric (which contains the science of yantra) paths and between the process of worship and attainment. Initially, in a tantric's practice, specific ceremony is effected, absolutely linked to the astronomical and astrological sciences. Therefore, charts (horoscopic) are analysed as to most opportune and auspicious times to begin a process. The tantric then creates a visualisation of being "central" or located in the inner middle of the spinal column, the centre of which is called "Meru". This is also called the "sushumna", through which the "kundalini" (coiled up energy or "shakti" within the chakra at the base of the spine) passes. This is the whole aim or ambition of the tantric, that his "kundalini" will ascend the "sushumna" and remain concentrated in the chakra between the eyebrows until the correct auspicious moment. At this time, success may be achieved by raising the kundalini to the crown chakra and ultimately brought forth to a destination beyond this world, leaving the material body in the flames of yogic fire.

TYPES OF YANTRAS

BHU PRISHT YANTRAS

Bhu means Earth and Bhu Devi is the name of Mother Earth. Accordingly they are made from materials found within the earth, as the name implies. There are two subdivisions. The first is raised yantras which include the bija mantras and vern mantras. The second is carved yantras.

MERU PRISHT YANTRAS

Raised, with a wide base, thinner midsection and peaked top in the shape of a mountain.

PATEL YANTRAS

Carved, in the shape of an inverted mountain, making it the opposite of the Meru Prisht yantra.

MERU PARASTAR YANTRAS

These are of the "Meru" mountain shape, but cut, rather than raised.

RURAM PRISHT YANTRAS

Have tortoise shell tops on a rectangular base.

These five types of yantras are classed according to the different puja (worship) conducted. Each has a separate and distinct purpose to gain a particular objective for the aspirant. Some yantras are worshipped in temples, some worshipped by individuals at home and some are worn on the body (usually of triangular or rectangular shape) either around the neck, the arms, or kept close to the body in another location. According to how the yantras are used they are further classified into seven divisions, as follows:

SHARIR YANTRAS

There are seven of these yantras, one for each of the "chakras". They are worn on the body and each has its own mantras. Chanting these mantras bestows various benefits to the aspirant.

DHARAN YANTRAS

These yantras are also worn on the body and include particular rituals producing different results.

ASANA YANTRAS

These yantras are positioned under the asana (sitting place) during puja. They are said to bear their fruit more quickly than other yantras and therefore are generally placed under the foundations of homes and temples, sometimes even under the worshipped deity of the home or temple, to bring the favourable results in a fairly short span of time.

MANDALA YANTRAS

These yantras are created using nine people to participate in the puja. They arrange their sitting places in the form of the yantra. One participant sits in the centre, another to the north, north-east, east, south-east, south, south-west, west and one north-west. The aspirant in the centre position offers the puja of the "Ishat" mantra and the eight others also chant individual specific mantras at the same time.

PUJA YANTRAS

These yantras are installed, whether in temples or individuals' homes, while puja is taking place. There are different yantras to serve various desires. They may be for different religious deity worship, or for the different planets in our solar system. The worship and installation of these yantras is of five basic steps:

1   Before the performance of the puja, the yantras are installed as icons, or worshipable deities. The yantras are drawn numerically and while offering the puja, the names of the respective "devas" (according to the numbers) are chanted throughout the mantras.

2   In the centre of the yantra is written the name of the particular deva being worshipped, then the puja is performed.

3   Either the first word of the mantra, the bija mantra, or the full mantra is written whilst preparing the yantra itself.

4   A carving, painting, or photograph of the deva and worshipable deity is attached to the yantra before beginning the puja.

5   Full-colour pictures of deva or worshipable deity are applied to the yantra.

CHATAR YANTRAS

These yantras are not placed upon the body, but kept in the pocket, or under a turban (or hat).

Darshan Yantras

These yantras are generally found in temples. "Darshan" means to take advantage of the association with a deity or other representative form of God, or His devotee. It is said that if an aspirant sees them during the morning hours, they will be benefic in awarding success. These are greatly "purified" yantras and are installed in great historic temples such as the temple of "Lord Jagannath, Balarama and Subhadra" in Jagannath Puri (also called Puri).

WRITING YANTRAS

There is a very definite system of writing yantras, and the methodology, as well as the specific pattern must be utilised and adhered to if the yantra is to be effectual. The aspirant creating the yantra must sit facing a particular direction, depending on the yantra and its use. There are different materials used in the making of different yantras. If done properly then the desired effect will be manifest.

There are different directions for drawing the lines within the yantra. If the yantra is for a positive purpose the lines are drawn beginning from the east and toward the west. On the other hand, yantras for overpowering enemies, or death-inflicting yantras, are drawn beginning from the west toward the east. Lines drawn for progress in specific actions are drawn from the north toward the south.

It is also extremely important that an auspicious time is chosen to make the yantra. Yantras for positive and good causes should be drawn early in the morning. Yantras for peace (shanti) are to be drawn at midnight. "Videshan" yantras (made for creating disputes or differences between people) should be drawn at midday. "Maran" (death-inflicting yantras) must be drawn in the evening. "Uchattan" (yantras to keep an enemy distracted and away from home) are to be drawn in the afternoon. Yantras such as "Vashikaran" (yantras to bring another person under the aspirant's control), are to be done before noon.

There are even exact hours at which time it would be most

auspicious to make the yantra in order to gain the most powerful effects. Different hours of the day or night are ruled by different planets and are thus proper for making specific types of yantras. I will list the types for the times governed by different planets as follows:

JUPITER

Yantras done for positive reasons, such as curing disease or for higher love and spirituality.

VENUS AND MERCURY

Yantras for successful business progress, keeping your own counsel, or yantras meant to control others.

SUN

Yantras for gaining favours from government, gaining personal power and meeting with important people.

SATURN

Yantras for inflicting death, or controlling others.

MARS

Yantras for legal difficulties, defeating an enemy, death-inflicting yantras, or, again, for controlling others.

MOON

Yantras for love and affection between a man and woman, or for general sexual attraction.

There are many different materials used for creating yantras, a common one being various forms of "Ashat Gandh" or powder made from different articles such as clay, minerals, or spices. Other materials, including pens made of jasmine, pomegranate wood (or the branches of other trees or bushes), or bird feathers may be used, depending on the particular yantra. I have not delineated these as they are all but impossible to obtain in western countries and, as the reader can see by now, it is a painstaking, exacting process to do correctly. As it must also be done by a qualified person (rare, even in India in this day and age) and as this book is for informative purposes only, I think that listing the materials used for drawing different yantras would have no practical purpose.

Finally in this section I would advise having a yantra inscribed in metal, for this is the most durable material.

YANTRA PUJA (WORSHIP)

As already mentioned, it is a prerequisite that puja is offered according to very specific rituals and by a qualified person, in order to benefit from the yantra. If this is not followed the yantra will be ineffectual. The steps for this worship are as follows:

1 Using both hands, flowers should be offered to the yantra while chanting the bija mantra. Remember that each yantra is representative of an individual "deva", or worshipable deity, so the aspirant must meditate on this particular form.

2 Holy water is next given up to the yantra. Generally this is water from the Ganges river.

3 Sandalwood paste or chandan (clay from a holy river) is then bestowed upon the yantra.

4 Garlands of flowers should be tendered, together with individual flowers and unhulled rice grains. The garlands should be placed upon the yantra.

5 This is followed by the burning of incense, and subsequently by the lighting of the ghee (clarified butter) lamp while the correct mantras are chanted.

6 Fruits are then proffered, along with betel nuts and leaves.

7 "Aroti" and "pradakshina", which are ceremonies in which the yantras are propitiated, follow.

8 Lastly prayers, then flowers offered again at the end, with all humility and sincerity, by the aspirant.

SPECIFIC YANTRAS

In this section I will delineate some different yantras, along with the methods of worship and mantras to be chanted during the pujas. I have neglected to include mantras and instructions for most yantras that are used for evil or controlling enemies and others. The reasons are obvious as I do not want to promote this science for anything but good, be it on a material or spiritual level.

You can find the diagrams of each mentioned yantra within this chapter. I will speak about "nava-graha" (planetary) yantras, but their individual illustrations are to be found in the planetary/astrological section later in the book.

SHRI YANTRA

This yantra is said within the vedas to be of the greatest general use and has prime importance. It is reputed to give fulfillment of ambitions for power, financial gain and influence. It also will give popularity to politicians, military officials and monarchs who desire to be loved by the people.

Mantra: *"Om Sharing Haring Kaling Haring Sri Mahalakshmaya Namaha".*

This yantra, also called "Sri Chakra" can be found in all south Indian temples and most individuals' homes. It is often used when the sun is badly afflicted in an individual's horoscope as the sun represents the physical body, and the eternal soul. "Surya Namaskar" (worship of the deity of the sun planet) must be performed for one week. The yantra is best inscribed in gold, silver, or copper, and once puja has been completed should be worn on a Monday morning.

BAGALA MUKHI YANTRA

This yantra is generally used within the mantra categories of stambhan, vashikaran, or uchattan. It should be prepared at a time when the planet Mars is at maximum strength and effect. It gives protection of the physical body from accidents, helps one to attain successful results in important academic examinations and is said to help overcome adversaries in, for example, arguments or legal challenges.

Mantra: *"Om Haring Bagla Mukhai Namaha"*

This mantra must be chanted 1500 times a day for 45 consecutive days to the presiding deity goddess Bagla Mukhi. The yantra may be drawn on bronze with turmeric, or inscribed into gold, silver, or copper. The puja is started on a Tuesday using yellow beads, garments and flowers. The worshipper must sit on a yellow-coloured mat or special sitting place and must remain vegetarian and celibate during the duration of worship. One last astrological point is that this worship should not be started if the moon is in the 4th, 8th, or 12th house from the natal sign's position.

KALI YANTRA

This yantra is said to grant fulfillment of all material desires including wealth, homes, and so on. It is often used to counter malefic effects of Sani (Saturn), as this planet is more often than not responsible for suffering, misfortune, and unhappiness during life. The yantra should be prepared at a time when Saturn's rays are more benefic than usual.

Mantra: *"Om Karing Kalikaya Namaha, Om Kapalinyai Namaha"*

This mantra must be chanted 10,000 times while meditating on and worshipping goddess Kali. Worship must be performed using rice and ghee (clarified butter). This yantra is said to give a long life-span and used as a cure for high blood pressure, paralysis, accidents and diseases of the nervous system. The yantra should be written on bronze, or inscribed in gold, silver, or copper.

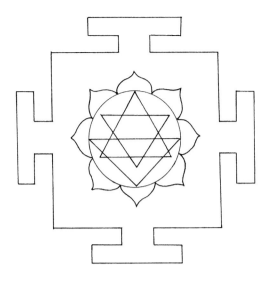

SHRI BHAIRON YANTRA

This yantra is said to bring good fortune and the fulfillment of any desires. It is used for improving impoverished conditions of life and for vashikaran or maran categories. The worship is only to be done at night, for fulfillment of a specific desire. The deity is "Bhaironji" who must be offered a particular type of alcoholic beverage. The food offerings are different depending on the day of the week the puja is performed. Always offered are jalebis (powdered milk and sugar formed into a pretzel shape and fried), toasted papdums, gram (chick peas) and apples. The following are added according to the day:

Sunday: use rice which has been boiled in milk rather than water

Monday: sweetballs made from milk

Tuesday: ghee and ghur (date sugar)

Wednesday: milk curds and sugar

Thursday: basen ladus

Friday: toasted gram flour (made from chick peas or garbanzo beans)

Saturday: urad dahl pakoras (urad dahl dipped in flour and fried)

Mantra: *"Om Haring Butkaya Apadudharanaya Kuru Kuru*
                           Butkaya Haring Om Swaha"

This mantra must be chanted 1000 times daily for 41 days. It is used for self-protection, relief from poverty, and falls into vashikaran and maran categories.

There are certain stipulations according to the uses as follows:

Vashi Karan

For influencing others the Bhairon mantra is chanted 10,000 times at a river bank, or within the jungle. It is to be done on a Thursday morning at sunrise.

Maran

I will give no instructions on performing maran mantras or ritual as these are death-inflicting and I do not wish to assist anyone desiring to perform such nefarious actions.

Relief from Poverty

The Bhairon mantra should be chanted 10,000 times while facing the west and only during the night-time. A lamp containing mustard oil should also be lit.

Protection

A different mantra is used as follows:

> *"Om Haring Bhairave Bhairave Thekarhar Maang*
> *Raksha Raksha Hoong Phut Swaha"*

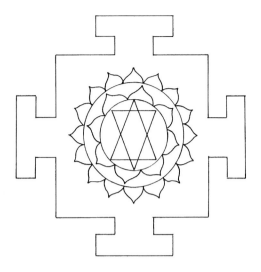

SARASWATI YANTRA

This yantra is said to give great intellect and the attainment of knowledge. It is also for success of artists and musicians. Uses are also known to be for curing insanity or other mental problems. Goddess Saraswati is worshipped by girls to gain the blessings of a good husband and satisfying marital relationship, as well as by married women for satisfaction within the conjugal relationship with their husbands.

Mantra: *"Om Sri Vidya Dayeni Sariswatiya Namaha"*

This mantra must be chanted 12,500 times a day for 40 days, then on the 41st day 20,000 times while performing sacrificial worship. The yantra must be sprinkled with Ganges water, kesar tilak (certain type of material for marking on the forehead of the practitioner) applied and a ghee lamp offered along with various fruits and flowers. After the 20,000 mantras on the 41st day milk sweets should be given to virgin girls. The yantra is to be worn on a Thursday. The aspirant must keep vegetarian and observe celibacy.

SRI GANESH YANTRA

This yantra gives fulfillment of desires, achievement of all ambitions and removes impediments from the way of endeavour. Actually Lord Ganesh is always worshipped before major pujas and sacrifices asking Him to remove impediments from the way of proper execution of the puja and also before beginning new endeavours of any type. This is a most important puja and either a deity of Ganesh, picture, or yantra can be utilised. The yantra can be made of gold, silver, or copper. Note that the swastika is a sign belonging to Lord Ganesh and is always found on this yantra. The yantra itself is made of six closed triangles, a centre triangle and central "bindu".

Mantra: There are 3 different mantras that may be used:

1   *"Om Haring Sharing Galo Gang Ganapatye Var Vard Sarvjanam Me Vashmanaye Swaha"*

2   *"Om Haring Sharing Galo Gang Ganapatye Var Vard Sarvjanam Me Vashmanaye Thatha"*

3   *"Om Gang Ganapatye Namaha"*

The puja should go on for a total of 30 days, chanting the mantra 1000 times daily. Offerings must include cow's milk, honey, coconuts and flowers.

MRIT SANJIVANI YANTRA

This yantra is said to be protective against disease, as well as bestowing wealth, fame and fortune upon the aspirant. It may be written or inscribed in copper or silver. Once worshipped and purified the yantra may be placed in a temple or shrine, or worn upon the body.

Mantra: There are 2 mantras which may be used as follows:

1   *"Om Joom Sah — Palay Palay"* *(place person's name in —)*

2   *"Om Hon Jung Sah — Jivae Jivae Palay Palay Sah Joom Hon Om"* *(place person's name in —)*

The mantra must be chanted for 45 days, 1000 times a day. In the puja offerings of incense, coconuts and flowers must be included. On the last day, a sacrifice should be performed saying the mantra 10,000 times with offerings of cow's milk and curds, rice cooked in milk, sugar, various kinds of fruit, mustard and "durba grass samadha" of banyan and palasa trees. The catech plant should also be included.

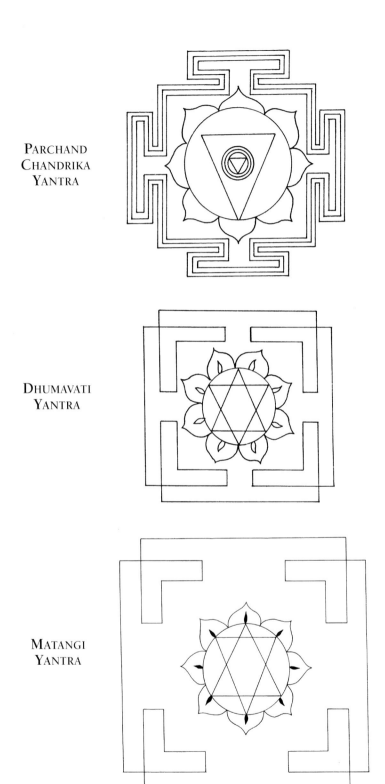

PARCHAND
CHANDRIKA
YANTRA

DHUMAVATI
YANTRA

MATANGI
YANTRA

64

Continued on page 9

THE CHAKRAS

SAHASRA DALA
KAMALA

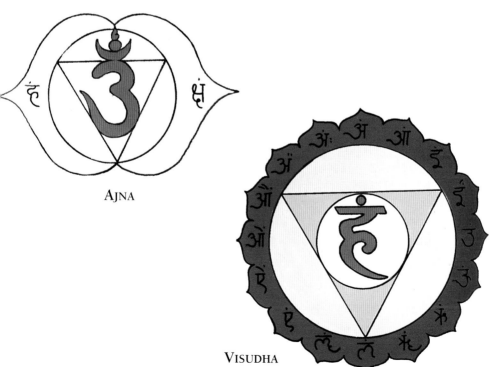

AJNA

VISUDHA

ANAHATA

MANIPURAKA

SWADHISTANA

MULADHARA

YANTRAS

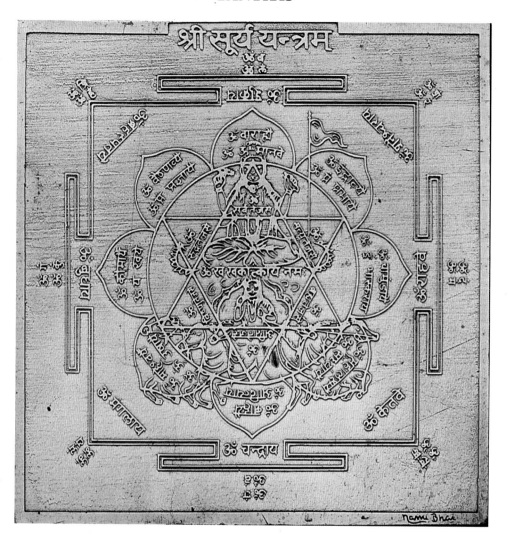

SUN (SURYA) YANTRA

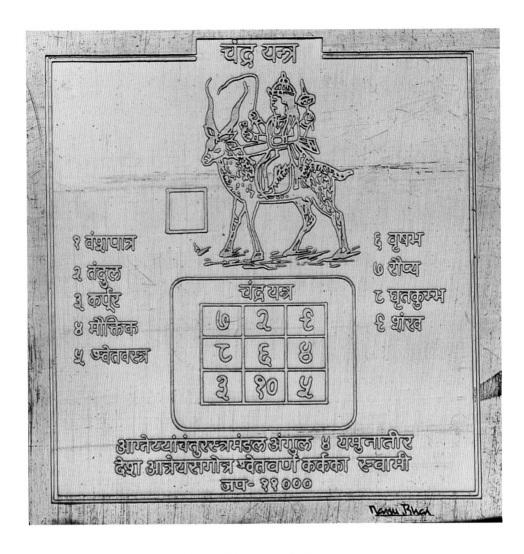

MOON (CHANDRA) YANTRA

संगल यन्त्र

१ प्रवाल
२ गेंहू
३ मसूर
४ लालवृष
५ गुड़

६ सुवर्ण
७ रक्तवस्त्र
८ कण्हेरपुष
९ ताम्र

मंगल यन्त्र

८	३	१०
६	७	५
४	११	६

लक्षिणे त्रिकोणमंडल अंगुल ३ अवंतिदेशोद्भव
भारद्वाज गोत्र रक्तवर्ण वृश्चिककमेषका स्वामी
जप-१००००

Mars (Mangala) Yantra

69

ANOTHER MARS YANTRA

MERCURY (BUDHA) YANTRA

JUPITER (GURU) YANTRA

१ चित्राम्बर
२ श्वेताश्व
३ धेनु
४ हीरा
५ रौप्य

६ सुवर्ण
७ तंदुल
८ सुगंध
९ घृत

११	६	१३
१२	१०	८
७	१४	९

पूर्व पञ्चाकोण मंडल अंगुल ९ वृष - तुलाका
स्वामी भोजकटदेश भार्गवसगोत्र श्वेतवर्ण
जप - १६०००

VENUS (SHUKRA) YANTRA

शनि यन्त्र

१२	७	१४
१३	११	९
८	१५	१०

१ माष
२ तिल
३ तैल
४ कुलित्थ
५ महिषी

६ लौह
७ श्यामधेनु
८ इन्द्रनील
९ श्यामवस्त्र

पश्चिमे धनुषाकार मंडल अंगुल २ सौराष्ट्र
देश काश्यपगोत्र मकर - कुम्भका स्वामी कृष्णवर्ण
जप - २३ ०००

Nanu Bhai

SATURN (SHANI) YANTRA

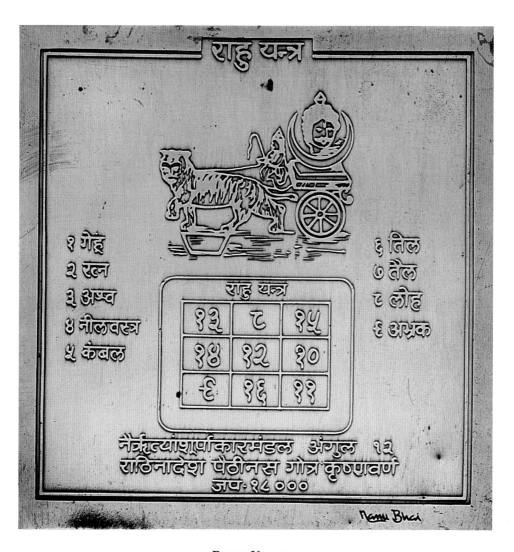

RAHU YANTRA

KETU YANTRA

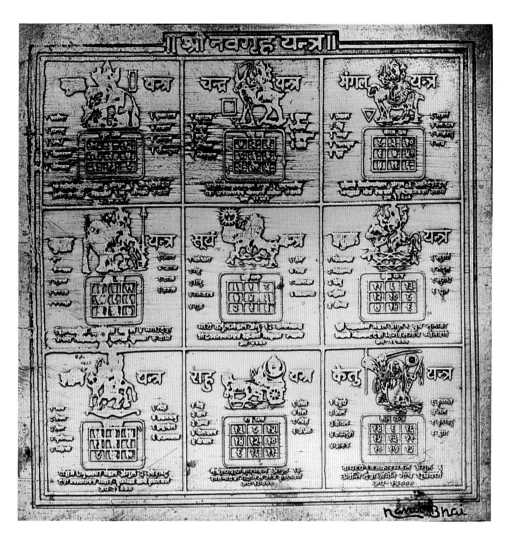

PLANETS (NAU-GRAHA) YANTRA

GANESHA YANTRA

SHIVA LINGA YANTRA

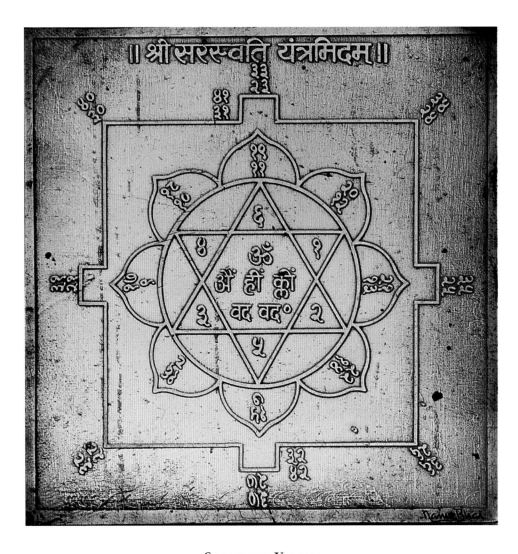

SARASWATI YANTRA

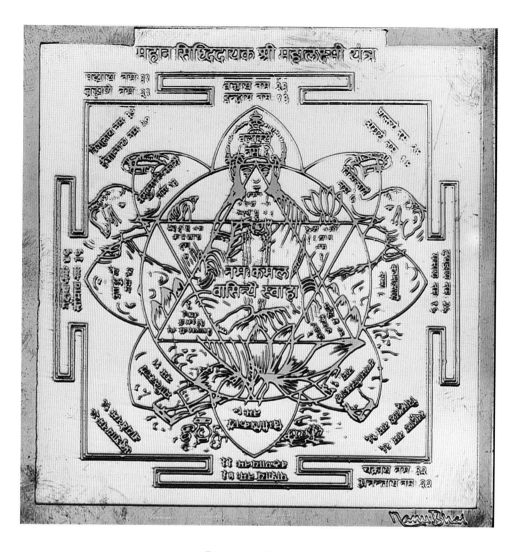

LAKSHMI YANTRA

DURGA YANTRA

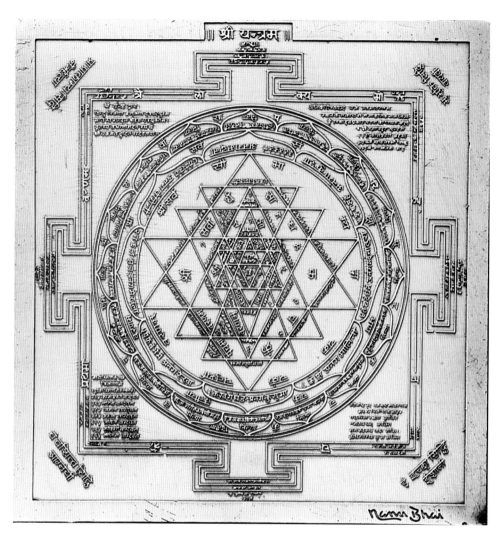

S<small>RI</small> Y<small>ANTRA</small>

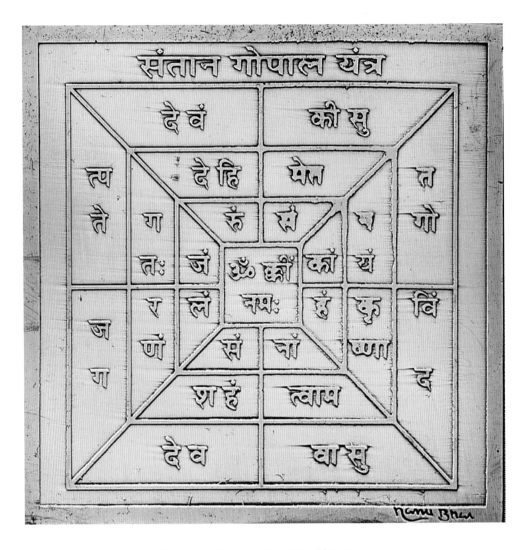

SANTAN GOPAL KRISHNA YANTRA

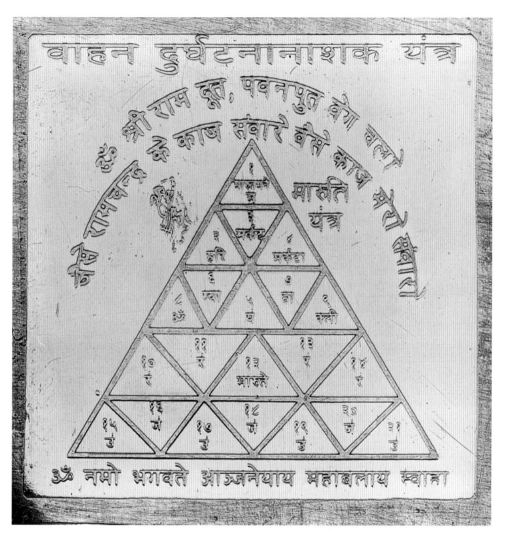

YANTRA FOR PROTECTION WHILE TRAVELLING

ANCIENT ASTROLOGICAL YANTRA

depicting animal signs S. India, courtesy Acharya R. C. Sharma 'Vyakul'
S.R.C. Museum of Indology Jaipur, Rajasthan, India.

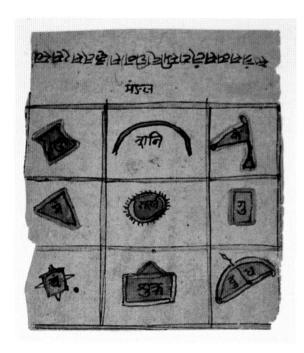

ANCIENT YANTRA

India, Courtesy of Acharya R. C.
Sharma 'Vyakul' S.R.C.

ANCIENT YANTRA

depicting animal signs N. India, courtesy Acharya R. C. Sharma 'Vyakul'
S.R.C. Museum of Indology Jaipur, Rajasthan, India.

Fabulous Gems

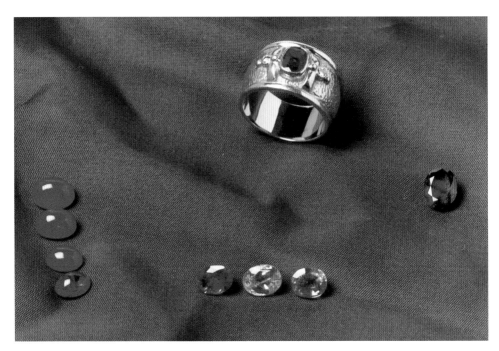

Rubies

Red Garnet

RED SPINEL

NATURAL PEARLS

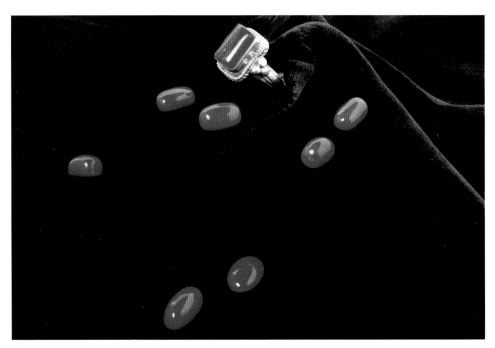

RED CORAL

EMERALDS

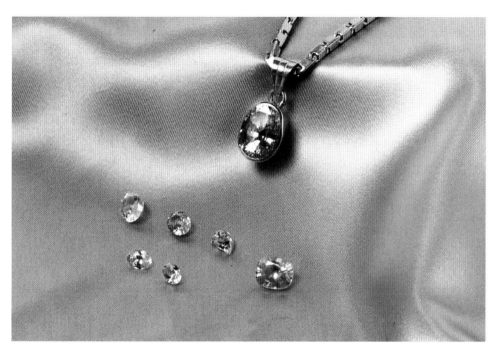

YELLOW SAPPHIRE

CITRINE QUARTZ

DIAMOND

WHITE SAPPHIRE

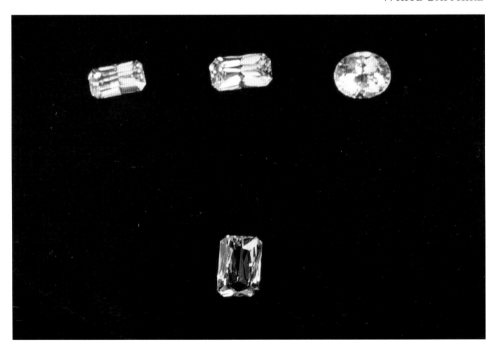

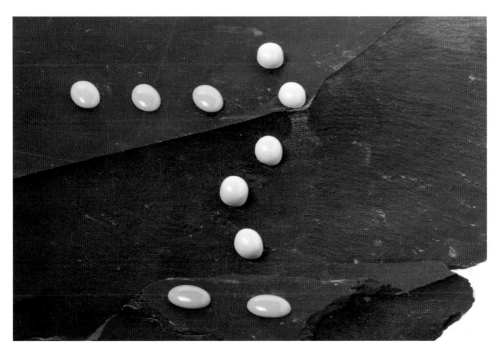

NATURAL TURQUOISE

NAVARATNA (9 GEM) PENDENTS

BLUE SAPPHIRE

AMETHYST

HESSONITE

CATS-EYES

The author and Acharya R. C. Sharma 'Vyakul' of S.R.C. Museum of Indology Jaipur, Rajasthan, India.

The author with the young man who provided us with the Copper Yantras photographed in this book, beside his shop at the Hanuman Temple in New Delhi.

The author purchasing natural gemstones in Jaipur Rajasthan, India.

Also pictured his dear friend Abid who insured authenticity of all gemstones.

Continued from 64

PARCHAND CHANDRIKA YANTRA

This yantra is said to bring relief from poverty, remove difficulties and to gain the birth of children. The yantra may be written or inscribed in gold, silver, or copper.

Mantra: *"Om Sharing Kaling Haring Aying Vaj Vyrochaneye Houng Houng Phut Swaha"*

This mantra must be chanted 10,000 times. In the sacrifice "bilwa" wood and ghee, as well as red flowers must be used. Offerings must include sweetened rice boiled in milk, dried fruits, lamp and incense.

DHUMAVATI YANTRA

This yantra is for success in all endeavours and for some people provides spiritual upliftment. The deity "Dhumavati Devi" is not known to many. She is old, fat in body and her back is bent. She wears dirty clothes, has dry hair and fierce-looking eyes. The aspirant must wear only loincloth during worship and it should be done in a far-removed place. The yantra should be written or inscribed in gold, silver, or copper.

Mantra: *"Dhoong Dhoong Dhumavati Thatha"*

This mantra must be chanted 10,000 times in complete solitude in the forest or in a cremation ground. The aspirant must fast and observe complete silence for 24 hours, wearing wet clothing and a turban on the head.

MATANGI YANTRA

This yantra is for gaining eloquent speech or musical expertise. The presiding deity is "Sri Mantangi Devi". The yantra is written or inscribed in gold, silver, or copper.

Mantra: *"Om Haring Matangaya Namaha"* (chant 10,000 times) then,

"Om Haring Kaling Houng Matangaya Phut Swaha" (repeat10,000 times)

MAHALAKSHMI (OR KAMALA) YANTRA

This yantra for the goddess Lakshmi brings fortune, wealth and general prosperity. It is said that all material desires may be fulfilled by chanting the mantra.

Mantra: *"Om Sri Mahalakshmiaya Namaha"*

Mantra to be chanted 10,000 times and puja performed offering incense, lamp and flowers.

MAHAMRITANJE YANTRA

This is another name for Lord Shiva and is extremely auspicious. It is said to bestow good health, wealth and all good fortune upon the aspirant. It is also said to cure disease and to be protective against ghosts or evil disembodied living entities.

Mantra:

"Om Hoong Joong Om Bhurbhava Swah
Om Triamakam Yajamaha Saugandhim
Pushtivardhanam Diyoyona Parchodhyat
Urvarukmev Bandhananmrityomu mamritamat Swaha
Bhuva Bhu Om Sah Joon Houng Om"

This mantra must be chanted 1000 times a day for 45 days. The yantra should be inscribed in copper or silver. With puja, incense, lamp, flowers, fruit and coconuts should be offered as sacrifice as is done with Sri Yantra, chanting the mantra 10,000 times.

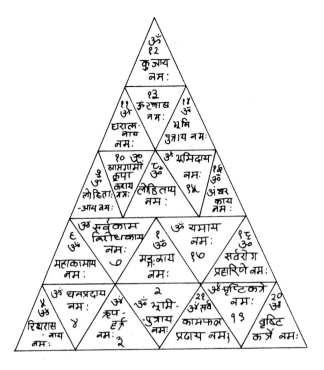

MANGAL YANTRA

This yantra is said to be an extremely fast-acting and powerful one. It brings relief from debt and stops bad temperament. It cures high blood pressure, protects from accident and is said to help anyone recovering from an operation. It is used for worship of Hanuman and the presiding deity of the planet Mars. It is inscribed in copper and made of 21 triangles enclosed within one large triangle. Within each triangle are imprinted names of Lord Mangal.

Mantra:	There are two mantras as follows:
1	*"Om Karang Karing Karoong Sah Bhumaya Namaha"*
2	*"Om Karang Karing Karoong Sah Bhumaye Namah Sah Karoong Karing Karang Om"*

Worship should be performed on a Tuesday and puja should include the offering of flowers and sweets made from rice or ghur. The aspirant must chant the mantra 1008 times. They must be vegetarian and observe celibacy throughout the day.

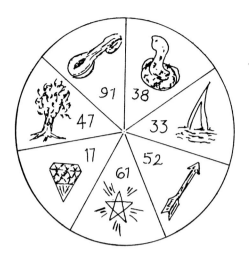

KARLA SIDDHI YANTRA

This yantra is said to bring about success in personal ambitions and provide all-round well-being. Its composition is of a circle, divided into seven equal portions, with a different drawing and numeric figure in each section. The drawings and numbers are:-

1 Snake with number 38:
Gives knowledge and wisdom.
It is also said to heal those in diseased condition.

2 Ship with number 33:
This is said to give courage to the individual and success in all endeavors, regardless of any impediments.

3 Arrow with number 52:
This gives protection against the "evil eye" and dangers surrounding the aspirant and/or his family.

4 Sun with number 61:
This gives good finances, personal power, and influence over others. It also bestows audience with superiors, political favours, and fulfillment of any desires.

5 Jewel with number 17:
This gives good health, wealth and general material prosperity.

6   Tree with number 47:
This insures the successful progress of all family members at present and in the future.

7   Vina (stringed instrument) with number 91:
Promotes harmony, happiness and is said to bestow personal confidence.

The yantra should be inscribed or embossed in copper and, after worship and purification, should be placed in the shrine at home or at the temple. It is noted that the total numeric value of all the numbers adds up to 339.

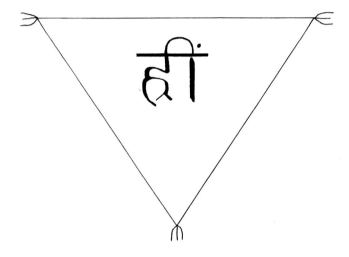

VASHI KARAN YANTRAS

These yantras are for gaining the love and affection of a person whom the aspirant desires. The yantra may be inscribed in gold, silver, copper, or stainless steel. It is either worn around the neck or kept elsewhere on the person.

Mantra   *"Om Daridrani Cintamani Gunanika
Janmajabadhao Nimanganam Dastram Muraripu
Varahasya Bhavati"*

This mantra should be chanted for a duration of 55 days, 1000 times daily. For puja the aspirant sits facing the north and hot milk is offered.

NAVA-GRAHA YANTRAS

"Nava" means nine and "graha" means planets, so these yantras are for propitiation of negative effects of planets or to increase beneficial planetary influences. Puja must be performed and mantras chanted as with all yantras. Again the aspirant must observe vegetarianism, refrain from using oils, and eat before sunset on the day of the specific puja.

The yantras may be written or inscribed in gold, silver, or copper. The yantras may be placed in a sacred place in the home, or made into talismans to be worn around the neck.

All mantras for the individual planetary yantras will be given in the individual planet's section within the planetary, astrological/astronomical section of this book.

There is also a combination of all planetary yantras in one single yantra for balancing all planetary effects. For this the "Navgraha" mantra may be chanted 1000 times a day for 45 days for purification of the yantra thus:

"Om Surye Namaha, Chandraye Namaha, Budhaye Namaha, Brihaspataye Namaha, Mangala Namaha, Shukraye Namaha, Shaniaye Namaha, Rahuaye Namaha, Ketuaye Namaha, Nava Grahaye Namaha"

Besides the geometric yantras there are "numerical yantras" for each planet. Each is based on a root number. A square is drawn or inscribed and divided into 9 equal parts (3 vertically and 3 horizontally). A number goes into each of the nine squares, with the planet's "base number" in the top middle square. All the numbers within the yantra added in any direction vertically, horizontally, or diagonally will add up to the same total sum. Examples of the numeric yantras for the nine individual planets are shown on the next page. The Geometric yantras for planets are shown in the colour section.

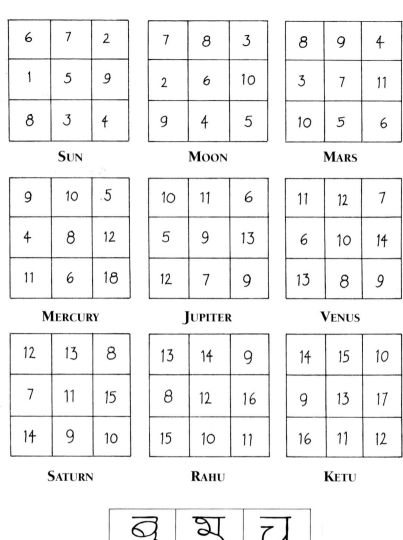

6	7	2
1	5	9
8	3	4

SUN

7	8	3
2	6	10
9	4	5

MOON

8	9	4
3	7	11
10	5	6

MARS

9	10	5
4	8	12
11	6	18

MERCURY

10	11	6
5	9	13
12	7	9

JUPITER

11	12	7
6	10	14
13	8	9

VENUS

12	13	8
7	11	15
14	9	10

SATURN

13	14	9
8	12	16
15	10	11

RAHU

14	15	10
9	13	17
16	11	12

KETU

NAVA-GRAHA YANTRA

GEMSTONE THERAPY

From time immemorial gemstones have been used by all cultures of the world. Their inherent beauty is second to no other material in the mineral kingdom. The word "gem" itself refers to something of an exquisite or superior nature. We refer to something of great quality or rarity, or even to special people at times, as "gems".

Today's science of gemology gives much information about the physical properties and chemical composition of gemstones, but gives no information of their "healing properties". They are extremely powerful tools to aid in balancing the physical, psychological and spiritual sides of life. This is necessary in order to keep oneself in proper order. The information I will give in this section is mainly from the Vedic viewpoint. This has been tried and tested for thousands of years and found to be accurate. The vedas have the greatest wealth of information on the metaphysical properties, as well as the physical properties, of gems and their correct application to enhance the lives of human beings.

THE HISTORY OF GEM THERAPY AND PLANETARY GEMOLOGY

Modern science recognises the potencies of gems in their technological uses, such as the use of crystals in watches, computers, and lasers. However, their subtle uses to cure disease, balance human emotions and infuse other potencies to the wearer are not recognised by western science and medicine. Thorough study of this subject has shown that the Vedic uses of gemstones in astrology and medicine have been proven by the experiences of countless people, both in ancient and modern times. The science of planetary gemology is used as a most effective healing tool within the eastern, or sidereal, system of astrology. Over a billion people throughout Asia and the world take advantage of this system to counteract imbalances throughout their lives, whether they be physical, mental, or spiritual.

In the histories of the Indian (of India), the Greek, Egyptian, as well as the Jewish cultures, gems were valued for their abilities to heal and also to enhance the lives of the wearers. Our Western system of birthstones traces its origin to the Breastplate of the High Priest, also known as the Breastplate of Aaron. In the Bible, Moses gave specific rules governing the "Breastplate of Judgement" which was set with 12 gems. Each gemstone was engraved with a name of one of the tribes of Israel. Through archeological research and excavations we find that man has always collected gemstones and had some knowledge of their uses and potencies. There is evidence of systematic mining in Egypt over 7,000 years ago, as well as in the Oxus Valley of Afghanistan.

However, no other culture had such extensive knowledge of the use of gems as did the ancient Indians in their scriptures. The Vedas contain the most complete storehouse of knowledge of gems, their description, potencies and prescriptions for effective usage. The instructions on their uses and prescriptions are found especially in the texts of the "Jyotish" and the "Guruda Purana." They give detailed descriptions of the uses of gemstones as remedial measures to counter imbalances in an astrological horoscope by the wearing of gems on the body, as well as the uses of gems in preparing elixirs and medicines to be taken internally.

Kings and queens wore gems on their crowns originally for the occult powers they imparted, rather than as a show of personal wealth. Gemstones were used as a basis for directing the subtle forces of nature, to increase the wearer's powers and abilities to achieve desired goals. Such desires included wealth, influence and popularity, preventing physical disease and averting disasters.

Gems were said by the ancient rishis and seers to be able to avert negative influences of planets and to increase positive ones. The colours and vibrations of specific gemstones directly correspond to the colours and vibrations of various planets in our solar system. Everything in the universe is influenced by and sensitive to colour.

The degree of influence they have on people is dependent upon the particular colours' emanations and absorption rate. The gems create their effect by both the absorption and reflections of the vibratory rays. They are extremely sensitive and contain radioactive crystals which can increase the cosmic rays received by the planets. When worn as rings or pendants they actually create an electromagnetic field around the person, but just as electricity works differently according to the particular equipment it is used to run, these rays work differently in different bodily constitutions.

Energy is the composition of the elements of nature as vibrational rays and wavelengths. When gemstone therapy is utilised the gems pick up and transmit a specific wavelength to the body. The body in turn transforms these rays into chemicals and elemental particles it can use to better function both on the physical and emotional levels.

The different planets and their gemstones will be discussed at length in this section. The gems are incredible repositories of their cosmic powers and their force is always positive. However, care must be taken that the correct gemstones are worn. Gems should be recommended by a qualified vedic astrologer, tantric, or ayurvedic practitioner as their effects are powerful and can cause detriment if incorrectly applied.

THE CURATIVE AND SPIRITUAL POWERS OF GEMSTONES

In the same way as medicines cure a disease by cumulative vibrational qualities, gemstones can counteract afflictions caused by the negative planetary effects. There are also medicines made from gems' ashes (bhasmas) and powders (pisthis) which have been used to cure disease by taking internally. The results have been astounding and referred to as "the ancient editions of modern isotopes".

There is also a method of placing a high-quality gem in a solution of diluted alcohol and placed in darkness for approximately 7 days, which allows the vibratory force of the gem to permeate the alcohol solution. This solution is then used as medicine. The gemstone loses no potency so this medicine may be made again and again with the same gem.

Another process is to place a gem in water in a glass jar in the sunlight.

This will allow the water to absorb this vibratory force, helped by the rays of the sun. A qualified ayurvedic doctor can mix different gem waters or tinctures for use by patients.

Furthermore, there are hidden potencies of another nature within gemstones. Such potencies may be unlocked by clairvoyants to see into other realms and to increase spiritual growth of the "higher self". In readings by the well-known clairvoyant "Edgar Cayce" he was adamant about the efficacy of gemstones for physical, mental, or spiritual benefits. He also stated that gems will not affect all people the same way and, therefore, a qualified person must make the diagnosis for application of a gem.

The human body is made up of the seven colours of the rainbow. Whenever there is a lacking within the body of any of these colours disease becomes evident. These colours are stored within gemstones in great abundance and are never depleted or used up, even after many years. As it is necessary to have a basic understanding of the science of light and colour therapy I will discuss these at some length before going further into the application of gemstone therapy.

LIGHT THERAPY

SUNLIGHT AND HEALTH

To understand colour therapy we must first understand the benefits of sunlight, which is the sum total and source of all colour. Each element has its own wavelength of colour. The main wave of colour within oxygen is blue, that of hydrogen red. When sunlight is absorbed by the body it is split up into its component colours. The different shades of colour are each produced by a different wavelength . As we have discussed in the section on "sound vibrations" the sound waves must be "in tune" to be in harmony. In this same way colours must be "in tune" to create harmony within the body for use as a therapeutic aid. There have been dramatic results from the use of colour in the treatment of disease.

It has been undeniably proven that exposure to sunlight is

necessary to maintenance of good health. It is mentioned in all ancient medical texts and sunbathing has been a treatment dating back to ancient times. The effect of light and heat radiation upon the metabolism is well-known by modern medicine as well. The cells become stimulated and promote greater elimination of waste through the sweat glands, and this produces an increased influx of blood. This makes for both better elimination of waste and absorption of nutrients.

It is evident how much healthier a person looks when exposed to regular sunlight, than those who live in climates where they get little or no sunlight for a large portion of the year. Lack of sunlight can cause "anaemia" as there is a decrease in the red blood cells and haemoglobin when there is no exposure to sunlight. Notice, also, how certain diseases, such as flu, infect the body much more easily during winter in climates where there is reduced sunlight.

Sunlight also slows or stops the growth of bacteria. I had an experience of this after a motorcycle accident many years ago. I had badly burned the calf of my leg and went daily to have the dressing and bandages changed, which was a painful process. After 3 days of this I decided to remove the bandages and just keep the wound exposed to the air and sunlight. By the end of the day the wound had begun to dry up and produce a light scab. Within a few days there was a scabby shell over the wound and it healed quickly after that. I had no further need of the doctor's changing of the bandages, nor the antibiotic cream given me.

Sunlight vitalises the human body, especially the skin. The sunlight is a combination of thermal (heat) rays and electromagnetic (frequencies of colour) rays which will enhance the growth and overall well-being of every part of the human organism.

It's important not to overexpose ourselves or we run the risk of burning, which will eventually cause abnormalities in the cells. Ultraviolet light is necessary to good health. Plants would wither and die without it, but we must be careful of how much we absorb. Everyone is different, so each person must find out their limits according to their sensitivity and resistance. Generally light-skinned persons can take less ultraviolet light than those with darker complexions. Get enough to promote good health and a feeling of well-being and increased strength.

VIBRATIONS OF LIGHT AND COLOUR

Colour, as we have said previously, are light waves of specific lengths. In modern times Sir Isaac Newton, credited with discovering the law of gravity, also found that when sunlight was passed through a prism seven distinct and separate colours were observed. These are the colours of the spectrum which are red, orange, yellow, green, blue, indigo and violet. These colours are visible in nature in rainbows or the polar lights.

Light is simply radiant energy which is visible to our eyes. The vibrations vary in size and vibrations of light less than 32 impulses per second are invisible as well as inaudible. The speed at which light travels is 186,000 miles per second. The electromagnetic spectrum is made up of a range of wavelengths that can be as large as hundreds of miles in length to as small as a thousandth of a millimetre.

The variations of light, heat and colour are in direct proportion to the variance of size of these wavelengths. Although extremely short wavelengths may be invisible, they still have colour, it's just that our eyes cannot pick it up. No medium is necessary for transmission of light rays, as is necessary with sound. They easily travel through space.   Modern physics classes colour according to wavelength, measured in "angstrom units" (A.U.). One angstrom unit is approximately one hundred-millionth of a centimetre. The approximate range of wavelengths of colours is as follows:

Violet	=	4300-4600 A.U.
Blue	=	4700-5000 A.U.
Green	=	5000-5500 A.U.
Yellow	=	5800-5900 A.U.
Orange	=	5900-6000 A.U.
Red	=	6000-6700 A.U.

There are many different types of electromagnetic energy sources and the waves of the electromagnetic spectrum have many varied uses. Some are positively used while other electromagnetic radiations may be dangerous. Here is a list of the most well known:

Cosmic rays, which are very short rays, are the ones we are concerned with in gem therapy, as they bombard the planet earth from outer space.

Gamma rays, used to treat some cancers, are given off by radioactive materials such as radium.

The x-rays used to take pictures within our bodies are thought to also cause cancers.

Ultraviolet rays which tan our bodies (from the sun), are used for photography and can destroy moulds and bacteria.

Visible light, originating from the sun, other stars and incandescent light bulbs allows our eyes to function.

Infrared (short) rays (from a great heat source) are used to take pictures in total darkness.

Long rays, also from heat source, are used for cooking.

Radio waves of a high-frequency oscillating circuit transmit sounds.

Very high frequency television waves transmit both sound and pictures.

The very long waves of alternating electrical current generate light, heat and power.

Colour and sound also both radiate energy. All living beings radiate energy, although these emanations are invisible to most of us, yet some living things, such as fireflies or glow-worms do emit visible radiation. Both colour and sound vibrations, unlike most of those mentioned in the previous paragraph, may be used without harmful side-effects to treat many physical and emotional disorders. In the next section we'll look at the impact of colour on the physical body, as well as the psyche.

COLOUR THERAPY

It has long been known that the energy wavelengths of colour can have a significant effect upon a person's health, psychological condition and general well-being. Different ones have very definitive effects upon our muscular and nervous systems. The medical profession discovered long ago that some colours relax people, some stimulate them, some seem to instigate a positive mental state and some seem to bring on depression. Both hospital workers and patients have been positively impacted by proper use of colours. Schools and factories have also improved productivity of students, teachers and workers by using particular colours.

Hotels try to use colours that seem friendly and comfortable. Even airlines choose colours to give good reflection of light, less feeling of claustrophobia and even to reduce the chances of "air sickness".

The colour red stimulates; green relaxes and promotes feelings of well-being; black can be a depressant; blue is calming for the emotions. Indeed, blue colour has been found to be good for patients recovering from surgical operations and, in mental hospitals, it's been shown to have a quieting effect on patients who have histories of violence. Bright yellows and oranges have been found to make recovering patients more positive and cheerful, greatly speeding their recovery due to an increase in their own desire to get better.

In a university in Australia it was found that students would be more attentive and gain better test scores by viewing slides in at least two colours during lectures, rather than black and white. We were recently told that an athletics director at one university painted one of their two dressing rooms red and one blue. The red one would be used for pep-talks to the football team (as red is stimulating) and the blue one for resting, as this colour promotes relaxation. When it came to home games they would use the red dressing room, while giving the visiting team the blue one, for obvious reasons!!

It has been found that colour can be used to restore physical vitality and depleted energy to organs of the body. This is certainly not a "new age" discovery, either. Pythagoras experimented with the effects of colour on health. Colour therapy was used not only in the golden age of Greece, but in Egypt's "healing temples of light". There are many practitioners of colour therapy, especially in England, who can confirm the dramatic positive effects upon the health of their clients. If the body is healthy, being given the proper diet, exercise, exposure to sunlight, and so on then it should naturally filter out needed colours from white light as necessary. However, if health is not optimum then the colour needs to be supplied to the body in some way.

Phototherapy, or exposing the body to coloured lights, has been used to treat illnesses and it has been found that certain glandular functions respond to specific colours. The secretions of the glands become stimulated, which in turn gives help to particular parts of the body. It was found that by treating specific organs through colour therapy the endocrine system was stimulated, the lymphatic system promoted better drainage and thus bacteria and rotten tissue were flushed from the body. As a result, accumulations of toxins within the body were also eliminated.

Sunlight in Food

"Photosynthesis" utilises the energy of the sun to synthesise carbohydrates from the carbon dioxide in the air, water and soil. What occurs is that the plant takes the sun's energy and changes it into a chemical energy. The chemical energy then converts carbon dioxide and water into protein, carbohydrates and fat. You might say that the chlorophyll of plants is their "blood".

The vast majority of the foods we eat should be grown above the ground as they carry the benefits of the sunlight they were exposed to during growth. Much of today's diet in the west is filled with nutritionally deficient food. Not only is this due to eating the flesh of animals, which is riddled with chemicals, hormones and other poisons, but certain preservatives used in the food industry interfere with natural properties of vegetables grown outdoors, or destroy the active ingredients in fats.

Vitamin D, available through the sun, is absolutely essential to good health. We can absorb it directly through the skin by exposing ourselves to the sun. Animals and birds also require it, but many actually have to get it by licking their fur or feathers after being in the sun, as their coats don't allow penetration. Vitamin D is not the only vitamin found in "solarised" food. Not only have other vitamins been found, but they've been linked to certain colours. Yellow is connected with vitamin A and most yellow foods are rich in this vitamin. Vitamin C is lemony-yellow colour and actually most yellow and green foods contain C. Vitamin B-12 is associated with red, vitamin D violet, vitamin K indigo and vitamin E scarlet. One of the best way of absorbing colour is through vegetables and fruit grown in the sun.

Though many people are not aware of the effects of colour, still it acts, just as you may not understand how the electricity is working to power the electrical appliances, yet they are still operating. There are many ways of positively utilising colour therapy through our clothing, the decor of the rooms we live and work in, using coloured lights and, best of all, from natural sunlight, as its rays nurture most living beings during the course of their existence here on earth.

Of course, one of the absolutely most effective ways of receiving the benefits of colour to a magnified degree is through gemstone therapy, which is the central subject of this section of this book.

PLANETARY GEMOLOGY

Different gemstones are said to receive their potencies from the cosmic energies of various planets. Vedic astrology and the Ayurvedic system of medicine tell us that certain planets can have effects on bodily organs and parts of the body. The planets are also said to have effects on our minds and subtle parts of our consciousness. In addition, their specific positions in the horoscope indicate (to a duly qualified practitioner of this great science) the path of destiny.

"Sidereal" astrology is used as a method of diagnosis for prescribing the gems. This system is far more precise and accurate than the system of "Tropical" astrology practised in the west for the reason that it is based on fixed positions of stars and constellations of stars, whereas the western system is based on the relative positions of the sun and the earth. The earth's orbit around the sun changes slightly from year to year, so the tropical system of fixing the point of 0° Aries at the point of vernal equinox (first day of spring) means the signs of the zodiac change position from the fixed stars and constellations of the same names. Being based on the sidereal zodiac, in vedic astrology we use the signs of the zodiac "as they are". Their positions were the same thousands of years ago as they are today.

This makes the calculations and predictions made by the sidereal astrologers far more accurate in determining strengths and weaknesses, as well as the direction of individual destiny. This is not to say that the western tropical system is of no value. It is very useful, especially for personality profiles and psychological considerations of a person, but the vedic system is far more accurate for predictive purposes as well as giving accurate information in all other areas of personality, and so on.

It should also be noted that gemstone therapy may not be applied to the tropical positions. Gem therapy is a powerful tool and remedial measure. In some instances wearing the wrong gem can cause serious physical and/or mental problems. Indeed, gemstone recommendations should only be accepted from a duly qualified vedic astrologer, planetary gemologist, or ayurvedic practitioner well-versed in this science.

How Gems Are Formed and React

Gems are formed over a period of thousands or millions of years through intense heat and tectonic pressure within the earth. They form in crystals of the most elemental forms of matter. They have the potency to absorb, reflect and radiate different frequencies of light. They are crystalline forms of energy, highly sensitive and radioactive. When worn on the body, gems transfer their energies in the form of ions which react with the electrolytes in the cells of our nervous systems.

The electromagnetic forces of the gemstones have specific reactions with the electromagnetic energy of the body producing various unique results. Again I must stress that users therefore be extremely careful to note the experience of a practitioner recommending the usage of gemstones, for improper usage can cause serious malefic effects.

MEDICINES MADE FROM GEMSTONES

In planetary gemology the concern is more with the method of wearing gems next to the skin, than with the medical preparation of gem elixirs and tinctures taken internally. The preparation of gemstones into "bhasma" (gem ash) and "pisthi" (powders of pearl or coral) are effective if recommended by a qualified ayurvedic doctor and obtaining a quality product for use. The products are available in India, but are rare in the U.S. or other western countries due to legal constraints, so I've decided not to give too much information on a subject that most readers will probably not have an opportunity to use.

There are also methods of making "gem water" and "gem alcohol" for medicinal use. Gem water can be easily made using a quality gemstone. If the gem is of an inferior quality it cannot be used for this purpose. Only the pisthis and bhasmas can be made using less than superior quality gems.

Water conducts heat and electricity, as we all know, and gemstones are electrolytes. When a gem is placed in water it ionises the gem. If the water is drunk it will help the electrochemical balance of our body's electromagnetic system. Colours are frequencies, but still may be considered chemical, therefore the water will be chemically changed through the light of the gemstone.

The gemstone should be kept in water overnight, then rinsed in cow's milk and again with water before use. It may be placed in a jar of water and placed in some sunlight for 2-4 hours, or kept in the water overnight. This "gem water" should be split into 3 parts and used morning, midday and at night. This water should not be stored more than one day as it loses potency.

Gem alcohol can also be made. It takes longer to make, about 12 hours, but can be stored, unlike the gem water. The alcohol used should be 90 to 100% spirit alcohol, the same as used in making homeopathic medicines. The gem is kept in water overnight, rinsed in milk and then water in the morning, then placed in a glass jar containing the alcohol. It should be kept somewhere where there is plenty of daylight, but not directly in the sun. The gemstone is kept in the alcohol for 12 hours, at which time it is ready for use as a medicine. It is generally administered in a dose of 10-12 drops, placed in less than half a cup of water. The gem alcohol is then stored in a box in a cool, dry place. The box should be lined with the same colour as the gem used to make the alcohol.

The therapist prescribing gem medicines must be familiar with the relationships of different gems to the seven dhatus, (body tissues) as well as the different parts of the body. The ayurvedic principle is that the practitioner understands which, within the three bodily humours, ("vata" or air, "pitta" or fire and "kapha" or earth/water) has become aggravated, treats the disturbance and thus once more helps the body to regain its correct chemical balance.

GEMSTONE TREATMENTS

Once a person receives a recommendation for wearing a particular gemstone it can be purchased from a dealer of gemstones or a jeweller. It should be noted that the gems must be of natural origin and must not have been treated with heat or irradiation in a laboratory. Such treatments are widely used in the industry to improve the colour or clarity of stones, thus making them more saleable. Although this may make a usually less attractive stone more pleasing to the eye, it effectively negates the stone's inherent energies, rendering it useless for therapeutic applications.

Almost all rubies and sapphires are "cooked", as it is called in the trade, together with most topaz, members of the quartz family, such as amethyst and citrine, spinels, garnets, tourmaline, peridot and a host of other gemstones. This practice has been going on for a long time and the "gem treaters" have become so advanced in their work that it is very difficult to discern. There is no loss in value, indeed the monetary value is generally increased by improving the gemstone's visual qualities.

Natural gems are getting rarer and it's important that the buyer looking for a "healing gemstone" either be an expert gemmologist, or know the person they are buying from, including their qualifications to examine gems for treatment.

"Synthetic gems" (man-made under laboratory- controlled conditions) are useless for gem therapy. Synthetic or natural gems that have been heat-treated may have some therapeutic value in regards to colour therapy, but just as much benefit could be obtained by wearing coloured glass, so why spend money on a gemstone for this purpose? Coloured lights and clothing would be just as effective from a viewpoint of colour therapy. Gemstone therapy has power and influence over the body and mind far beyond this.

I have been in and around this business all my life and, as a qualified gemologist, know that even most jewellers and dealers cannot easily tell the difference. In actuality most really don't care either way, as they look at gems as a business for adornment or fashion, not as tools to effect healing. In our family we go to great lengths to obtain natural, untreated gemstones and must travel the globe in search of them.

Another treatment which is used, mainly with emeralds, is oiling the stones. Each gemstone species has what we call in gemological terms R.I., or refractive index. This is a scale used in an instrument called a "refractometer" which measures the angles at which light bends in various gemstones. In a gem which generally has many fractures or other imperfections (such as emeralds do), if an oil can be used to "fill" the fissures which has the same refractive index as the gemstone itself, the imperfections become almost invisible. When light hits the imperfections in the gem it bends at another angle, but if the cracks are filled with an oil (such as cedar oil or balsa oil which have almost the same refractive index as emerald), then the light will not change its course and the crack will not be seen. Eventually this oil seeps out of the stone and the stone will show the imperfections.

There are also less sophisticated treatments such as wax or plastic impregnation. These are to improve the appearance of the gemstone, generally used with stones cut in the domed or "cabachon" style, such as coral and turquoise.

As you can see it is important to purchase from a reputable person, as well as get the recommendation from a knowledgeable practitioner. I have had the experience that many astrologers recommend gems to clients, and also obtain them, yet do not have the gemological knowledge or experience to know how to examine the stone. As a result they may, inadvertently, cheat their own clients, as they are being cheated by unknowledgeable or unprincipled dealers.

I have personally had the unenviable position of having to inform a person that their gem is not what it's supposed to be when brought to me for gemological evaluation. Many times I've seen people who have bought gems in "source" countries and, not only was the stone either treated or a completely different gem than was purported, but it was of a quality so poor that it would cause harmful effects.

Gems are extremely powerful, as I've repeatedly stated and low quality stones can cause an opposite effect to that desired. Gemstones should always be "beautiful". This is their prime attribute. If a stone looks unattractive you can be sure it's not suitable for therapeutic purposes. If you cannot afford the high price of a good quality ruby, then it is much better to get a good quality rubellite (red tourmaline) or red garnet. However, the size would need to be somewhat larger in the substitute stones to compensate. The same goes for all gems. Choose fine quality in a substitute gemstone (generally referred to as "semi-precious") rather than a low quality primary gemstone.

CHOOSING AND WEARING GEMSTONES

Once a proper stone is obtained it may be set in either a ring or pendant for wearing on the body. The gem must be set in such a way that the stone comes into contact with the skin. It should be set just close enough to touch the skin, but not so close that it causes irritation by being pressed against the skin with force. Such unnecessary pressure will actually bruise the skin and flesh as gems are some of the hardest substances known to man. Gems should be set by themselves, as certain gems are incompatible and may cause undesired effects if set together in the same piece of jewellery.

There are exceptions in the case of specific talismans where certain gems are set together for a positive combined effect. A common example is the "navaratna". "Nava" means nine and "ratna" means jewel. Therefore, this is a specific piece (generally pendant as in a ring the stones are generally too small to be effectual) containing all nine gems for the nine planets, ruby, pearl, red coral, emerald, yellow sapphire, diamond (or white sapphire), blue sapphire, hessonite (gomed) and cat's-eye. Ruby is set in the centre and the other gems configured in a circular fashion around it.

There are also other talismans made with a gem and yantra on a specific shape or figure for the planets individually. They are difficult to make and I have rarely seen them in India, not to speak of the west! Accordingly, in the interest of giving information in this text which can be utilised practically, I am not describing them at any great length. The information I do give about the use of gem therapy can be used by anyone, once they have a proper gem prescription and obtain the gemstone needed.

It's also important to wear gemstone rings on the proper fingers. The forefinger (next to thumb) is the Jupiter finger and yellow sapphire is best worn here. The middle finger is the Saturn finger, so blue sapphire should be worn here. The "ring finger" (next to smallest finger) is for the Sun, Moon, and Mars so ruby, pearl, and red coral rings are best worn here. The smallest finger is the Mercury finger so this is the optimum place for rings of emerald or green jade. In palmistry the thumb is connected to the "mound of Venus". However, as we don't generally wear rings on the thumb, diamonds or white sapphire rings should go on a friendly planet's finger, either middle finger (Saturn), or the small finger (Mercury). The same goes for hessonite (or gomed) and cat's-eye.

Pendants are best worn at either the throat chakra or the heart chakra for maximum effect The gemstones must still be set so that the culet (bottom) of the stones contacts the wearer's skin.

The size of gems used is also an important factor. Most of the precious primary gems are "facet-cut" and transparent. These include ruby, emerald, diamond, blue sapphire, yellow sapphire and hessonite. They should be well over one carat and are better around two carats in weight. (There are five carats to a gram of weight). Pearls are chosen of a size and weight depending on body weight. Generally I have found that 5 carats is adequate. (Natural not cultured pearls are best.) Red coral generally needs to be around 8 carats, and cat's-eye between 3 to 5 carats. All are becoming rare.

Although some gems can be quite expensive, the exercise is often a one-time purchase and the gem can be worn for an entire lifetime. What other commodity can continue to be useful, effective and increase pleasure and well-being throughout the entire span of life?

GEMSTONES AND THE VEDAS

Since ancient times India has been a source of wealth coming from mother Earth. Even today, contrary to the belief of many westerners, it has more wealthy people than any country in the world. Gemstones and precious metals are more highly revered to store wealth than are stocks and bonds, in which westerners frequently invest. Gemstones and gold are undoubtedly the most highly-prized fruits of the earth. India's oldest text, the Rig Veda gives reference to their uses, which had a much deeper purpose than most people think of today. They were used for healing, and for spiritual reasons. Their use as an ornament was of secondary importance. Gems were known to increase the flow of different energies. Individuals would use them both for their own good, and in places where all would benefit from their energies, as in temples dedicated to God.

Gems are the life force of the mineral kingdom. In the Vedic texts on astrology, there is information on how the different gems are actually storehouses of the different energies radiated to earth by the other planets in our solar system. They are the means of connection between the earth and the other stars and planets. They are connectors between the physical energies and the subtle ones. Therefore their usage harnesses specific energies to help in various ways enhance the overall quality of life.

THE BENEFITS AND DETRIMENTS OF GEMS

During the Vedic times in India, only the largest and most powerful gems were used in the temples. Deities and altars were often inlaid with incredible gems that would cause man to marvel at their sheer magnificence. The Hindus, Jains and Buddhists alike used the finest of gems for these reasons. The sincere devotees of these faiths considered that the best things in God's creation should be offered back to Him. Using gems in their worship would bring spiritual energies into the world to the benefit of all. Instead of allowing the wealth of possessing these gems to bind them to this world, they would be used to glorify the Divine.

Unfortunately the greed of invading armies in India caused them to desecrate the Hindu temples and steal these most precious of jewels. The Muslims, British and Portuguese all committed this great offence and consequently the great amounts of knowledge, powers and potencies contained in them were lost. Because of the great power of these stones, their unlawful possession by man caused the possessors to become cursed. The stories of the calamities that befell people possessing them have been the subject of much conjecture and speculation. The "Hope Diamond," for instance, caused havoc in the lives of its owners, leading to its donation to the Smithsonian Institute in Washington D.C. in the hopes that the owners could escape any further effects of its curse.

Many of the British crown jewels were pillaged from the sacred temples of India and it is said that this was a factor in the demise of the British Empire. In India they say that part of these ill effects may be seen in the lack of sunshine in England, which has dreary, cloudy weather most of the time!!

For our purposes we are mostly concerned with gems that individuals can wear on their bodies. The benefits are many and I will give more of the individual stones' potencies for healing and balancing planetary energies in the planetary section. The detriments will only be felt if wearing a poor quality gem, or if wearing a gemstone which is incorrectly prescribed to be worn.

THE POWER OF GEMS

At the expense of repeating myself, gems earliest use was for healing and spiritual ritual. Their value as concentrated wealth came into play at a much later time. Although gems were rare and exhibited great beauty, the reason they were so precious was the power they imparted to their wearers. They are storehouses of power which is transmitted through contact with one's body. As I stated previously, kings and queens would have gemstones set in their crowns to obtain their potencies. They connected the monarchs with forces enabling them to rule guided by cosmic energies. Priests of different religions used gems in rings for similar reasons. Gems exhibit their power in a beneficial or detrimental way depending on how they are used.

Ancient cultures used gems and sound vibration to direct the subtle forces of nature. The occult power of gems is said to have caused natural calamities by improper usage, such as the destruction of Atlantis. They are said to have been the catalyst for moving the great, huge blocks of stone used to build the pyramids of Egypt.

The inherent powers of gemstones are recognised by modern science in the technological uses of crystals in watches, lasers, and computers, but the more subtle potencies, such as their ability to promote physical healing in the body, and their power to help balance human emotions, elude discovery by modern science.

"New Age" Teachings of Gem Therapy

There is a great interest in the west at present in the occult, and many different groups have sprung up with their own definition of the utility of gemstones. More often than not, they are lacking in a reliable origin of the teachings they accept in the area of gem therapy. Most of the "new age" teachings on crystals and gems seem to be from "channelled" information. For those of you unfamiliar with this term I will explain. A psychic, or medium, enters a trance and allows a disembodied being to enter their body, using the person's voice-box to impart some message or information. The person speaking through the medium is living on a non-physical dimension at present and may have been in human form fairly recently or maybe not for thousands of years. Just as there are all kinds of people in this world and on this physical dimension, there are different calibres of personalities living on "other" dimensional levels. I leave you to draw your own conclusions as to the doubts I, as an astrologer, planetary gemologist, and researcher on this subject, who depends on tangible , historical sources for the texts studied , may have.

On the other hand, the Vedic, or ancient Indian, science is based on 5,000-year-old texts and thousands of years of known experience. Gem therapy and its use to enhance people's lives is described in the ancient texts on "Jyotish" (translated as the "science of light" and refers to the vedic astrological science) and the "Garuda Purana", as well as others which can be relied on for authenticity.

From all my studies, the ancient uses of crystals in their "natural form", that is not at all cut or polished, are for healers or for directing subtle forces in other ways. For example we know gem crystals were buried in specific configurations under the foundations of temples, or other structures. The temples of ancient India, Israel and Egypt used this science, including the pyramids. Healers educated and trained in this method of healing, used wands and natural crystal shapes to redirect or replenish electromagnetic fields within the human body. Nowhere have I read of everyday people wearing uncut crystals for this reason. The method was gem therapy, using cut and polished crystals of superior quality gemstones.

My feeling is that those with a "commercial sense" see a good marketing gimmick and somehow the public just goes along with it without asking too many questions. As a trained gemmologist I have looked at many crystals which are supposedly naturally shaped in the earth and found them actually to be shaped on a "lathe" to look like the original, especially in the case of capped (with metal and decoration) crystal pendants.

Crystals are wonderful for purification of home environments and can be used to enhance plant growth, among other things, but we find nowhere in the vedas where crystals are recommended to be worn in their original shapes and formations.

THE BENEFITS OF GEM THERAPY

The proper stone can bestow fantastic benefits. There should be a strong meditation by the wearer of the results desired. Even in children, where the parents are the ones devoting all the mental energy, we have seen dramatic improvements. The use of pearls with young children has been shown to be effective in helping to calm hyperactivity. It seems to make them think with more clarity.

The practice of indiscriminate placing of gems on the body, especially this new age practice of gem crystals all over the body, is dangerous. Herbs or medicines would not be indiscriminately taken without consultation with a doctor or expert in that field, and the use of gems and crystals should be taken as seriously. Improper use of gemstones can short-circuit magnetic fields of the subtle body and can result in severe physical debility in some cases. Gems can also have an adverse effect on the mind causing mental problems and emotional dissatisfaction.

As I stated earlier, gems are also made into oxides for internal use, but it is a very slow, painstaking process to make them and there are currently few or no sources for this most potent of medicines in the west. However, there are knowledgeable practitioners of Vedic astrology and we can take advantage of their expertise to determine gems that will be of benefit to us when worn externally.

The medical and astrological uses validate each other. Different planets have influence on different parts of our bodies. A weak planet in the chart often manifests physically as a weakness in the part of the body affected by that planet's cosmic energy. Gems have the power to harmonise planetary influences. The gemstones for each planet are as follows :

Primary Gemstones

Sun:	Ruby
Moon:	Pearl
Mars:	Red Coral
Mercury:	Emerald & Green Jade
Jupiter:	Yellow Sapphire
Venus:	Diamond
Saturn:	Blue Sapphire

| Rahu: | Hessonite Garnet (Gomed) |
| Ketu: | Chrysoberyl Cat's-Eye |

Secondary Gemstones

Sun:	Red tourmaline, red spinel, red garnet, red zircon, sunstone
Moon:	Moonstone
Mars:	Red Jasper, Carnelian, pink coral
Mercury:	Peridot, green tourmaline, green zircon
Jupiter:	Yellow topaz, citrine quartz
Venus:	Colourless sapphire, zircon, or quartz, turquoise, white coral
Saturn:	Lapis lazuli, amethyst
Rahu:	Any golden grossularite garnet
Ketu:	Any other cat's-eye, tiger's-eye

The gemstone, once chosen, is set in metal for wearing on the body. Metal acts as the transmitter of the stones' potencies to the wearer. Different gems react better using different metals. Rubies, red coral and yellow sapphire and their substitutes should be mounted using yellow gold. Pearls should always be set in silver, as silver is cooling (while gold is heating) and pearls are most noted for calming or "cooling down" the mind or emotions.

Emerald, diamond, blue sapphire, hessonite and cat's-eye can use either yellow or white metals in different instances but generally white metals (silver, white gold, or platinum) are best. The most beneficial place to wear the most powerful primary gemstones is on the fingers as rings. The energy is most efficiently transmitted there by the nerve centres in the fingers. Different planets correspond to different fingers on the hand, as we have previously described and the most effective is to wear the gem on the proper finger.

Secondary gemstones may be worn as rings, bracelets, or earrings. Either primary or secondary gems may be worn as necklaces. The jewellery should be fashioned in such a way that light will pass through the stone to the body. This means that the piece must be open-backed and the stone must be mounted so that it comes into physical contact with the skin.

BIRTHSTONES

The origin of modern western "birthstones" can be traced to the days of Moses when he gave instructions about the "Breastplate of Judgement ." This is corroborated by the academic texts of the Gemological Institute of America. In the Bible, the breastplate is described as being set with 12 gemstones, each with an engraving of the name of one of the 12 tribes of Israel.

In the Book of Revelations, gems in the breastplate were described as being the foundation stones of the temple of the "New Jerusalem". The order that the 12 gems were given was used as the order for birthstones for the months. For no seemingly relevant reason the first of the birthstones was assigned to the month of March. Together the two lists are as follows:

March:	Bloodstone or Jasper
April:	Sapphire or Diamond
May:	Emerald
June:	Agate
July:	Turquoise
August:	Carnelian
September:	Chrysolite
October:	Beryl
November:	Topaz
December:	Ruby
January:	Garnet
February:	Amethyst

These stones were used as birthstones until August 12, 1912 when the American National Retail Jewellers Association (ANRJA) changed the list to stones which would be more advantageous commercially for the jewellery industry. Then, in 1938, the American Gem Society (AGS) adopted the new list, adding one additional stone, citrine quartz, to the list. In 1952 the list was once more changed and gained the approval of ANRJA, AGS, NJA (National Jewellers Association) and ASIA (American Stone Importers Association). This, then ,established the official list of birthstones that is still used today, as follows:

January:	Garnet
February:	Amethyst

March:	Aquamarine or Bloodstone
April:	Diamond
May:	Emerald
June:	Pearl, Moonstone, or Alexandrite
July:	Ruby
August:	Peridot or Sardonyx
September:	Blue Sapphire
October:	Opal or Pink Tourmaline
November:	Topaz or Citrine
December:	Turquoise or Zircon

The Jewellery Industry Council of America established this as the official list of birthstones. It is not hard to see that this list was arbitrarily created and has no astrological meaning. It has absolutely no correlation whatsoever to the astronomical/astrological signs of the zodiac. Since the sun changes signs every month around the third week , it is not possible to assign any stone to an entire month. In the western system of astrology, or the tropical system, the position of the sun determines the birth sign.

Really there is no other way of making a commercial system. It is only by the calculation of movements of the sun that birthdays can be used to choose a stone. The purchaser would have to know the positions of ALL the planets at the time of their birth to choose a gem any other way. The sidereal zodiac is "as it is", not a relative system based on relative positions of the sun and earth which is the case in the tropical zodiac. Accordingly, it is the position of the moon that determines the birth sign. Therefore in the east, and most especially India, people generally know at least the positions of both the sun and moon at the time of their birth. The majority had an astrological horoscope drawn up by their "family astrologer" when they were infants.

It is important to note that it is the sign of the zodiac that is the determining factor at birth, not the month in which one is born. Therefore the present birthstone system as we know it is only a commercial system for selling gems. It has no benefit at all, except to the wallets of the jewellery merchants.

The signs of the zodiac each have a planet that is the lord, or ruler, of that particular sign. Each of the planets also has a gemstone that vibrates and transmits cosmic energy. Therefore the only meaningful system of birthstones is according to the sign which the sun, or moon, tenants at the time of birth, although it is our opinion that choosing a stone according to the moon sign is best.

The list of birthstones accepted throughout India and all of Asia since ancient times is according to the position of sun, or moon, namely:

Sign of Zodiac	Ruling Planet	Birthstone
Aries & Scorpio	Mars	Red-Coral
Taurus & Libra	Venus	Diamond
Gemini & Virgo	Mercury	Emerald or Jade
Cancer	Moon	Pearl
Leo	Sun	Ruby
Sagittarius & Pisces	Jupiter	Yellow Sapphire
Capricorn & Aquarius	Saturn	Blue Sapphire

Serious wearers of birthstones must have a horoscope drawn up, or at least be able to use an ephemeris to find the position of the moon at their birth to choose appropriately. The sun changes signs approximately in the middle of the month, so use the 15th as the date, although in some months it may be a day or so earlier or later. At least this will show the reader how completely bogus the system in use in the west today really is. According to the sun's movements through the actual (sidereal) zodiac the dates of passage annually are:-

January 15 to February 14:	Capricorn
February 15 to March 14:	Aquarius
March 15 to April 14:	Pisces
April 15 to May 14:	Aries
May 15 to June 14:	Taurus
June 15 to July 14:	Gemini
July 15 to August 14:	Cancer
August 15 to September 14:	Leo
September 15 to October 14:	Virgo
October 15 to November 14:	Libra
November 15 to December 14:	Scorpio
December 15 to January 14:	Sagittarius

Combining Mantra, Yantra and Gem Installation

In the following section there are included instructions for ritual in the installation of gemstones for personal use. Often I have helped a client to obtain a needed gem and they gave it to another person they felt more "qualified" to install it. There are many Hindu priests or Tantrics who are well-versed in planetary sacrifices and can use the gem in this elaborate ritual and afterwards you may consider it ready for wearing. However, I feel that the person who is to wear the gem should be taking part in the ritual.

I always remember this phrase, told to me years ago, that "in healing, no one can do as much for you as you can for yourself". It is important to bring your "own" energy into play, as it is that which you wish to strengthen. Even if the ritual is performed by a priest the wearer should still chant the mantra at the correct time before wearing the gem for the first time. Especially in the west people sometimes get lazy and want someone else to do it for them. Take the time to do it yourself and you will find that the benefits will be vast. Not only will the ritual installation be empowering for the use intended, but your own feelings of self-confidence and faith in your own ability to help yourself will be greatly enhanced.

PLANETARY SECTION

RUBY - GEMSTONE OF THE SUN

THE POWER OF THE SUN

The Sun is the ruler of the sign Leo in the zodiac. It is exalted in Aries and in debilitation in Libra. Sun rules the nakshatras (constellations) of Karttika, Uttara Phalguni and Uttarashadha. Natural friends are the Moon, Mars and Jupiter. Natural enemies are Saturn, Venus, Rahu and Ketu.

The Sun's position in one's horoscope will indicate a variety of traits in an individual, both physical and psychological. First, we should understand what the sun represents in an astrological horoscope. The Sun is considered the ruler of our entire solar system. All the other planets orbit around it and are dependent on the Sun's energy for the existence of most life forms living upon them.

From the position of the Sun in a horoscope ,we can understand a lot about the person's physical appearance, although it is not the only factor. It represents the basic behavioural traits of a person as well, but again there are other factors that must also be taken into consideration. The Sun is the representative of father, so a competent astrologer should be aware of the parental status, traits and the relationship a person has with him. Even the length of the father's lifespan can be seen by the position of the Sun at the time of the person's birth. It can also be representative of the husband in a woman's chart.

The Sun gives us power through the vitamins contained in its rays, so the level of a person's physical power, or energy, is also determined by the Sun.

The Sun will also determine the amount of influence to be gained over others during his or her lifetime. The Sun is the king of all planets and is the supplier of light and heat to the universe, and therefore has more influence over life than any other planet.

Success in maintaining a healthy body, vitality, immune system and the willpower to achieve greatness in society is under the purview of the Sun. It gives life force, intelligence and prosperity. It is indicative of wealth, wisdom, good fortune and success in all worldly affairs. Our ambition and the ability to understand the physical and phenomenal world all come under the sun's control.

The Sun represents kings, government officials, people in government service and leaders. It represents wealthy or famous people, as well as those living in or connected with a church, temple, or religious institution. It also represents creative people like artists, actors, jewellers, gemologists, and merchant traders in gold. Doctors, nurses and those connected with the healing field are also ruled by the Sun.

The Sun, if well placed in the chart, can give great abilities in the categories I've mentioned, making a person cheerful, fortunate, and wise. If ill-placed in the horoscope it can indicate a myriad of physical as well as possibly mental or emotional problems, pessimistic attitude, humiliation at the hands of others and impoverished conditions of life. A strong Sun can give rise to fame in their area, field, or even the whole world. An individual would be virtuous, full of vitality and have the potency to instruct or command others in a proper way if the Sun is beneficially disposed. The Sun can indicate that a person's status in society increases steadily during their lifetime to a place far above that in which he/she was born.

If the Sun is afflicted in the horoscope, it may make a person too proud or egotistical. It may also indicate excessive arrogance or boastfulness. The Sun will reveal it's full influence between the ages of twelve and twenty-four years.

Of the physical body the Sun is ruler of the heart, head, lungs, liver, nervous system and skeletal structure. It indicates the right eye in a male and the left in a female. To fast on a Sunday is recommended if the Sun is weak in the horoscope.

THE RUBY

Ruby is the gemstone recommended to strengthen a weak Sun and to therefore offset the afflictions brought on by its weak position. Courage and will-power may be increased by wearing a good ruby. It will increase vitality and the ability to perceive things in a true and correct manner. It can help in developing spiritual insight, or looking within toward spiritual realisation.

On the physical side, it may strengthen the heart and help digestion and metabolism. It should be noted that rubies are so powerful that if worn by the wrong person they may cause physical or mental imbalances in the categories governed by the Sun. If in the horoscope the ascendant (rising sign) is Capricorn, Pisces, or Virgo it is recommended in general that one of the substitute gems for ruby be utilised instead. Red tourmaline, called rubellite, or red garnet may be substituted for ruby and will give the same effects, although with somewhat less potency.

A ruby should be of an even colour ranging from deep-red to other tones depending on occupation. A teacher, intellectual, or priest should wear a ruby of a pinkish-red colour. A ruler, administrator, or military officer should have a blood-red colour ruby. A merchant of any goods or produce, or one involved with banking or monetary instruments would wear a slightly orangey-red colour. An artist, clerical person, or skilled or unskilled labourer would wear a ruby of a dark purple-red colour.

The major sources of rubies are Thailand, Burma, Laos, Cambodia, India, Sri Lanka, Africa and Afghanistan.

GEMOLOGICAL CHARACTERISTICS OF RUBY

SPECIES:	Corundum
TRANSPARENCY:	Transparent to translucent
COLOUR:	Red to mixtures of red with pink, purple,orange and black
REFRACTIVE INDEX:	1.763 to 1.77
BIREFRINGENCE:	0.008

PLEOCHROISM:	Very strong dichroism
CRYSTAL SYSTEM:	Hexagonal
OPTIC CHARACTER:	Doubly refractive
SPECIFIC GRAVITY:	4.0
MOHS HARDNESS:	9
DISPERSION:	0.018
FLUORESCENCE:	Long-wave (weak to strong red)
VISUAL IDENTIFYING CHARACTERISTICS:	Hexagonal growth lines, rutile (silk) needles, fingerprint inclusions, straight colour banding

INSTRUCTIONS FOR INSTALLATION OF A RUBY

Ideally consider purchase of the ruby on a Sunday, Monday, or Thursday when the Moon is waxing. It should be mounted and installed for use when the Sun is in Leo and Pushya nakshatra. The other nakshatras ruled by the Sun (Karttika, Uttara Phalguni, and Uttarashadha) are also good times.

It should be at least 1.5 carats in weight and must be set in yellow gold with the back of the ring or pendant open, so the ruby actually comes into contact with the skin.

Once having the finished piece the following short ritual is recommended for further empowerment. On a Sunday at sunrise:

1) wash the ruby ring/pendant with water

2) rinse it with cow's milk

3) rinse again with water

4) place on your home altar (or in a sacred place), before a picture of the deity of the Sun (Surya) or a yantra of the Sun

5) light incense

6) meditate on the benefits desired from wearing the gemstone

7) repeat following mantra 108 times: *"Om Hring Hamsa Suryaya Namah Om"*

8) place ring on ring finger of hand, preferably the right

Pearl - Gemstone of the Moon

The Powers of the Moon

The Moon represents the mind and, accordingly, it indicates a person's thinking, feeling, and willing processes. It represents all things having to do with one's mother, as well as motherhood in women.

It is representative of interaction with the public, or public businesses, water, liquids and the tides of the sea, over which it rules. It also has dominance over the waters and liquids within our bodies.

Emotions and sensitivity may be understood by the position of the Moon in a person's chart. The Moon's nature is tender-hearted and wise. It rules peace of mind and gives a general sense of comfort and well-being. The Moon reflects understanding and sense of purpose, intuitive ability, sensuality, love for fine arts, music and jewels. It also rules our moods, emotions and sensitivity.

The Moon is also responsible for growth, fertility and impregnation or conception. It influences childbirth and memory and has great influence over travel.

A strong Moon in the chart will indicate a happy mental state, good mother, opportunities for travel over water and success in businesses having to do with the day to day needs of the public. It may bestow a wonderful social life and pleasure from different enjoyments if the Moon is beneficially disposed, or well aspected. A powerful Moon gives emotional strength, makes for good relations and love for others. It will give good intuition, purpose to life, an attraction for the fine arts and make a person attractive to others.

If the Moon is weak in the chart you may be subject to mental anxiety. There may be emotional instability and an inability to relate well to others. If badly aspected, the Moon can make one unfriendly and unable to share intimacy, or will cause you to lack contentment or peace of mind. An ill-placed Moon may make for inclinations to moodiness and feelings of depression, with an unclear mind. Depending on how severely afflicted it is there may be a tendency towards neurosis, hysteria, or insanity. It can make a person feel a lack of joy or satisfaction, therefore bringing about acute realisation of the sufferings felt in this material world. There may be indications towards ill health of the mother, or difficulties in social advancement.

Physically, an afflicted, debilitated, or otherwise ill-disposed Moon may indicate anaemia, a lack of body fluids or body weight, constipation and dryness of the skin. It can cause colds, fevers, bronchitis, intestinal problems, or even susceptibility to cancer. Organs, such as the lungs and kidneys, may also be weak and there may be menstrual or infertility problems in women.

The Moon is the ruler of the sign Cancer of the zodiac and is strong there in its own sign. It is most powerful, or exalted, in Taurus and fallen, or debilitated, in Scorpio. Jupiter, Sun and Mars are the Moon's natural friends. Moon is very strong in its nakshatras of Rohini, Hasta and Shravan. It is still quite strong in Jupiter's nakshatras of Punarvasu, Vishakha and Purvabhadrapada. It is also giving good effects when in Karttika, Uttara Phalguni, Ashlesha, Jyestha, Uttarashadha and Revati.

The Moon is auspicious for those born during the waxing of its cycle but causes difficulty if born during the descending cycle. It is always a benefic planet and is strongest from the tenth day of waxing to the fifth day of its waning. Its effects are powerfully felt in childhood, as Moon rules over this period of life.

THE PEARL

Pearl is to be worn to strengthen a weak Moon in the horoscope and may help to alleviate conditions caused by a weak placement. It has an extremely calming influence on the mind and increases feelings of love, and compassion for other people. The pearl may increase peace of mind and enable the practice of spiritual meditations with greater concentration.

On the physical side, the pearl may help balance bodily fluids and reduce heat in the body. The pearl can calm the nerves thereby decreasing feelings of anxiety. It is good for women in general and can help fertility, as well as help a woman deal with the stresses of motherhood.

Most people, especially in the west, are only familiar with cultured pearls. Although they can be quite expensive, especially in strands of good size, shape and colour, they are not anywhere near the potency of natural pearls. Let me explain the difference.

Pearls are said in the Vedas to come from eight sources. Seven of them are extremely rare and not to be found on earth in this day and age. They are "sky pearls" (from the sky), "cobra pearls" (develops within the hood of a cobra aged over one hundred years), "bamboo pearls" (found in the hollow of bamboo), "hog pearls" (found in the head of a hog), "elephantine pearls" (originates in the temple of a particular breed of elephant), "conch pearls" (found in a conch shell), and "fish pearls" (created in the womb of a fish).

All these have different powers and healing potencies attributed to them, but we have not known anyone possessing any of them. ("Raj Roop Tank" wrote in his book entitled "Indian Gemology" that he saw all of these pearls in the collection of "Dhanroop Mal", a very famous jeweller from Ajmer.)

The source of pearls with which we are all familiar are those produced by a mollusc (oyster). It starts with a tiny irritation within the shell of the mollusc, possibly a piece of sand or other foreign matter. The oyster, as a protective measure, begins to coat this irritation with two substances, nachre and conchiolin. The layers are coated one after the other, with the greatest part being the nachre. This is a "natural" pearl, meaning man has not induced the oyster to create a pearl. Most natural pearls have been long ago taken from the seas to the point that they are very rarely, if ever, found today.

Cultured pearls are the only pearls commercially available to the public. This is the process by which man induces the oyster to create a pearl. A piece of tissue is implanted within the oyster along with a round bead of "mother-of-pearl", cut from the shell. This bead is then coated (in the same way as with a "natural" pearl) with subsequent layers of nachre and conchiolin. After a certain time period the pearls are "harvested".

Generally this is done on pearl "farms", in the far east or the south Pacific. The south Pacific produces the largest pearls in white, silver and black colours. Other sources include the Persian Gulf, South America, India and Sri Lanka. Cultured pearls may be used to strengthen an afflicted Moon, but one natural pearl, worn either in a ring or pendant, is more effective than several strands of cultured pearls.

The only natural pearls we are still able to obtain, although in very limited quantities, are "keshi pearls". These are "accidental" naturals. Sometimes in the culturing process the mollusc rejects the implanted bead and forces it out of it's shell. Still, due to being irritated, it produces a pearl, but without the bead. Therefore the pearl is for all practical purposes "natural", being entirely made up of the pearl substances nachre and conchiolin. I have seen incredible results using keshi pearls for an afflicted Moon, and stock as many as I can get for clients, as the supply is getting less and less. This is because the farmers are getting better at "tricking" the oysters into making cultured pearls and they even have learned to "reimplant" the nucleus (the mother-of-pearl bead).

As with all gems you must know the source well to be sure. The only foolproof way of knowing if the pearl is cultured, or not, is by X-raying the pearl, which will reveal the nucleus, if there is one. If the pearl is drilled, it can be seen under magnification easily but, for healing purposes, PEARLS SHOULD NOT BE DRILLED. They should be set only in silver, so that the pearl comes into contact with the skin.

Moonstone may also be used as a substitute for pearl, although the potency is somewhat less powerful. If using Moonstone it should ideally be 8-10 carats in weight.

GEMOLOGICAL CHARACTERISTICS OF PEARL

SPECIES:	Pearl
TRANSPARENCY:	Translucent to opaque
COLOUR:	White, cream, yellow, green, blue, pink, silver and black
REFRACTIVE INDEX:	1.53 to 1.686
CRYSTAL SYSTEM:	Aggregate
SPECIFIC GRAVITY:	2.7
MOHS HARDNESS:	2.5 to 4.5
FLUORESCENCE:	Long wave (inert to strong) Short wave (inert to moderate)
VISUAL IDENTIFYING CHARACTERISTICS:	Orient, gritty (sandpaper-like) texture if rubbed against teeth

INSTRUCTIONS FOR INSTALLATION OF A PEARL

Pearls are best purchased on a Monday, although Sunday and Thursday are also suitable days. The Moon should be waxing and in one of the nakshatras of Rohini, Pushya, Hasta, or Shravan. Size is prescribed according to the body weight of an individual, but generally 4-6 carats in size has dramatic positive effects within 72 hours.

The pearl should be set in a silver ring, or pendant, so that it comes into contact with the skin. Once installed, if in a ring it should be worn on the ring finger of the left hand. The following ritual may be performed for empowerment. On a Monday evening after Moonrise:

1) rinse pearl ring/pendant in water

2) rinse in cow's milk

3) rinse again in water

4) place on home altar (or sacred place) before a picture of the deity of the Moon (Som or Chandra) or Lunar Yantra

5) light incense

6) meditate on desired benefits

7) chant following mantra 108 times *"Om Som Somaya Namah Om"*

8) place pearl on ring finger of hand, preferably the left, or pendant on a chain around the neck

RED CORAL - GEMSTONE OF MARS

THE PLANET MARS

Mars is a masculine planet, extremely fiery in nature. He is said to be the commander- in- chief of the planets of our solar system and is personified as the God of War. Mars has the nature of a warrior. The position of Mars in the horoscope shows the amount of energy a person has and how this energy is utilised. Therefore, Mars is the indicator of our physical and mental energy. He rules over determination, courage and bravery as well as leadership, self-confidence, forcefulness and physical strength. Competitive spirit, athletics and the martial or military arts are all categories of Mars. Mars presides over those in the food business, such as cooks and restaurateurs as well as policemen, soldiers, officers and generals.

Mars' natives are often short-tempered. They may be argumentative and usually love guns, explosives and all types of weaponry. They have mechanical and technical talents making them skilled as builders and engineers. Mars represents the real estate, or land and housing business, including the areas of construction, buying, selling, renting or building.

Mars is orderly and likes things arranged properly. He gives drive and determination, as well as purposefulness.

Those ruled by Mars are generally fiercely independent and can react with violence if they feel it is justified. It can also make a person rash, impulsive and insensitive to the opinions of others. Passion or sexual prowess is also shown by the position of Mars in the chart.

More often than not a powerful Mars will also make for selfishness. It can make for a willing participant in illegalities in business, as well as for fondness of secret or illicit sexual relationships. Mars can cause physical harm, such as burns and bruises and is always capable of doing harm as it is a very malefic planet. A strong Mars gives stamina, courage and determination, making a person constructive and energetic. If it is well-placed it makes those so fortunate to be capable of leading others and indicates success in all Mars categories. Mars shows his full effects between the ages of 27 and 32 years.

Mars is strong in his own signs of Scorpio and Aries, is exalted in Capricorn and debilitated in Cancer. In its nakshatras of Mirgishira, Dhanistha and Chitra it is also very potent. Mars is natural friends with Jupiter, Sun and Moon, is neutral to Venus and Saturn and enemies with Mercury, Rahu and Ketu.

If Mars is afflicted, or ill-placed, it makes for a waste of energy on worthless things. It may indicate physical harm or debility or make a person angry, cruel, or violent. It can make for aggressiveness, and a lack of proper manners or social skills. A weak Mars means the person will not have ambition, motivation, or the stamina it takes to achieve success. Anything beyond meagre advancement becomes very difficult and the individual is usually relegated to a lower status in society, or life in general.

Weak Mars may also make for a weak character, making them targets for mental and physical abuse. Physically, it causes a feeble immune system, poor appetite and a weak body in general. Wounds and injuries may be slow to heal and, in men, it is a cause of lack of sexual desire and vitality. Blood diseases, ulcers and fevers, as well as excessive burns and/or bruises may also be attributed to effects of this planet.

RED CORAL

Coral is made of deposits of calcium and secretions from the invertebrate "coral polyp". The deposits are built up in a structure resembling plants with branches. This creature generally lives in calm water and builds the corals in depths from 20 feet to as deep as 1000 feet. Red corals are this colour due to iron oxide within them and are generally found in depths of 100 to 150 feet. The shallower the water the darker the colour of coral and, obviously, the deeper the water the lighter the shades of colour found.

To strengthen a weak or afflicted Mars, wearing a red coral stone (best), or strand of beads is recommended. The deeper red it is in colour the more potency it will have. I have seen startling results from proper use of this gem, especially in the area of sexual desire and performance in men. Unfortunately this gem is becoming in short supply due to uncontrolled farming of our seas. Deep red coral stones especially have become extremely expensive when once they were plentiful and cheap.

Nowadays much of the red coral on the market has been dyed, so beware. It should have even colour and good texture, with no holes or cracks.

The wearing of this stone will increase vitality, courage and ability to work on things through to their fruition. Physically it is said to strengthen the immune system, the muscles of the body and the male reproductive system. Generally I recommend a red coral gemstone weighing 8 carats (a minimum of 6 carats) for ring or pendant, but ring is best. It should be purchased on a Tuesday, as this is the day of Mars, when Mars is in Scorpio or Aries (if possible) or in the nakshatras of Mirgashira, Chitra, Anuradha, or Dhanistha.

The sources of red coral are the Mediterranean, Persian Gulf, Red Sea, Africa, Australia, Taiwan and Italy, although it is becoming unviable commercially due to being in short supply. I have also been receiving some red corals from Tibet, giving me the understanding that at one time the sea came up to this mountainous country. Pink coral, red jasper and carnelian may be used as substitutes for red coral, having the same properties but in a lesser degree.

GEMOLOGICAL CHARACTERISTICS OF CORAL

SPECIES:	Coral
TRANSPARENCY:	Translucent to opaque
COLOUR:	red, pink, orange, white and black
REFRACTIVE INDEX:	1.486 to 1.658
CRYSTAL SYSTEM:	Aggregate
SPECIFIC GRAVITY:	2.65
MOHS HARDNESS:	3.5 to 4
FLUORESCENCE:	White coral only has weak to strong blue under either long or short wave
VISUAL IDENTIFYING CHARACTERISTICS:	Wavy parallel fibrous structure ,uneven fractures with dull lustre

Instructions for Installation of Red Coral

Red coral should be set in a ring or pendant of a mixture of copper and yellow gold. Ideally installation when Mars is in its own signs or the signs of a friend and in its own or friend's nakshatras, mentioned above, is preferable. The best piece of jewellery is a ring worn on the ring finger of the right hand. For more empowerment the following ritual may be performed before wearing for the first time on a Tuesday, one hour after Sunrise:

1) rinse coral ring/pendant in water

2) rinse in cow's milk

3) rinse again in water

4) place on home altar/shrine before a picture of the deity of Mars, or a Mars Yantra

5) light incense

6) meditate on desired benefits

7) chant following mantra 108 times: *"Om Bhom Bhomaya Namah Om"*

8) place ring on ring finger of right hand, or pendant on chain around the neck

Emerald and Green Jade Gemstones of Mercury

The Planet Mercury

Mercury, the planet of intellect, represents intelligence as well as communication of all kinds. It has a quickly changing and fickle temperament and, being the lord of Gemini, can give a dual nature. It may make a subject detached and independent, or an extremist. It is known as a "mutable planet" in that it reflects the attributes of planets it is associated with, being a "neutral" planet. It is representative of education and literary affairs and the communication of ideas, such as in advertising, sales, lecturing or teaching spiritual concepts. Its full effects are seen between the ages of 32 and 35 years.

Writers, lecturers, artists, sculptors (or people that use their hands in their profession) and teachers, as well as astrologers, accountants, office workers, traders and businessmen, more often than not will have a prominent or well-placed Mercury in their charts. Playfulness, enthusiasm and talkativeness are traits of Mercury's influence, in addition to independent thinking and appreciation of tradition. The ability to learn different languages, convince others, memorise and develop good business acumen come under Mercury's influence. Friendships and ability to learn things are due to Mercury's energies. It gives proficiency in the arts and the ability to do things quickly, or several things at one time.

Mercury is the ruler of the signs Gemini and Virgo of the zodiac and becomes exalted in its own sign of Virgo. It is debilitated in Pisces. Mercury is friends with Venus, Sun, Rahu and Ketu, neutral to Saturn, Mars and Jupiter. It is enemies with the Moon but does well in the nakshatras of Ashlesha, Rohini, Revati, Jyestha, Shravan and Hasta.

A strong Mercury gives good intelligence and a myriad of abilities under the categories mentioned above. Successful communicators of all types have a well-placed Mercury in their horoscopes, whether they be artists, business people, in the entertainment business, or involved with the media.

A weak Mercury may make subjects restless, fearful, or neurotic. When Mercury is ill-placed or aspected, it may cause a lack of intelligence or communicative skills, or a poor memory. It can make a person immature, foolish and childish. Feelings of insecurity and a lack of self control, leading to addictions and artificial dependencies, may also manifest from a poor placement of this planet. Physically it can show itself as weakness of the nervous system, anxiety, nervous digestion, or insomnia. It may cause bowel and elimination problems such as diarrhoea or constipation, difficulty digesting food, kidney disease, or respiratory problems.

Malefically disposed it causes sufferers mental or physical pain, or undue anxiety. This may vary from being too fearful and nervous to serious psychosis and lunacy.

EMERALD OR GREEN JADE

Emerald or fine green jade is recommended for strengthening a weak Mercury. It increases the powers of communication. Obviously this is important and necessary for business people and those in the various fields of communication, be they writers, speakers, or entertainers. Most people would agree that quality of communication is 90% of the determination to succeed in whatever endeavour they may wish to undertake.

Emeralds and jade are said to strengthen the nerves and, on the physical side, to purify the blood. It increases the flow of positive life-energy and so has been used by healers to further increase their ability to mend the body and mind.

It is most important that, to be most effective, the emerald has a minimum of flaws and a depth and intensity of colour. It is much better to use a very clear, flawless emerald of light colour, than to use one with many imperfections. Emeralds generally are flawed and most jewellers would say that these flaws insure a "natural" stone. That is not entirely true as synthetics are grown in laboratories with such advanced technology today that they can induce "natural-looking" flaws to be produced. In any case, the flaws interfere with the transmission of Mercury's cosmic energy and should be avoided.

"Oiling" of emeralds is also a common procedure, as I mentioned earlier before the planetary section. Actually ALL emeralds are put into oil right from the mines. If there are inclusions/imperfections, such as fractures that reach the surface, manufacturers or dealers can induce the oil to enter them by either putting the emeralds in oil and heating slightly, or those more technologically advanced use "vacuums" to get the oil into the stones. Since the refractive index (angle that light bends in a substance) of cedar oil (most often used) is about the same as that of emerald, it causes the imperfections to be invisible. This is a commonly accepted practice in the trade, so emeralds must be carefully studied to make sure of the quality.

Another practice, although it is considered cheating if not disclosed, is putting green dye into the oil to deepen the colour of the stone. One easy way to have a better look at the stone is to hold it gently with tweezers and submerge it in a glass of water. Looking through the glass at the emerald should reveal whether dyed oil has been used.

Sources of emerald are South America, most notably Colombia (the best in the world) and Brazil. There are also several countries in Africa (Zambian and Tanzanian are best),which, together with India, Iran, Pakistan, Afghanistan, Egypt and Russia are also sources.

Jade is of two types, jadeite jade and nephrite jade. "Precious" jade is jadeite, which is costly and comes in different shades of green, as well as lavender, white, red, blue and black. Only the green is used for strengthening Mercury. Nephrite generally comes in green, is common and not expensive. Jadeite is most effective, and should be of even colour, translucent (not opaque) and at least 5 carats. It can be dyed and also other materials, such as chalcedony, may look like and therefore passed off as jade. Sources for jadeite are Burma and China; for nephrite China, the United States and New Zealand.

Peridot and green tourmaline may be used as substitutes for emerald or fine green jade, as well as lesser qualities of green jade, although their potencies are lesser than the primary stones.

GEMOLOGICAL CHARACTERISTICS OF EMERALD

SPECIES:	Beryl
TRANSPARENCY:	Transparent
COLOUR:	Green, yellow-green and blue-green
REFRACTIVE INDEX:	1.577 to 1.583
BIREFRINGENCE:	0.005 to 0.009
PLEOCHROISM:	Weak to strong dichroism
CRYSTAL SYSTEM:	Hexagonal
OPTIC CHARACTER:	Doubly refractive
SPECIFIC GRAVITY:	2.72
MOHS HARDNESS:	7.5 TO 8
DISPERSION:	0.014
FLUORESCENCE:	inert to weak green under long or short wave
VISUAL IDENTIFYING CHARACTERISTICS:	3 phase and 2 phase inclusions (combination of solid, gas, and liquid material), calcite, pyrite or mica inclusions, tremolite needles, fractures

GEMOLOGICAL CHARACTERISTICS OF JADEITE JADE

SPECIES:	Jadeite Jade
TRANSPARENCY:	Translucent
COLOUR:	Deep green, apple green, lavender, white, blue, red
REFRACTIVE INDEX:	1.66 to 1.668
CRYSTAL SYSTEM:	Monoclinic, aggregate
SPECIFIC GRAVITY:	3.34
MOHS HARDNESS:	6.5 to 7
VISUAL IDENTIFYING CHARACTERISTICS:	greasy to waxy lustre

GEMOLOGICAL CHARACTERISTICS OF NEPHRITE JADE

SPECIES:	Nephrite Jade
TRANSPARENCY:	Translucent to opaque
COLOUR:	Dark green, bluish-green, white, black, grey, yellow and red
REFRACTIVE INDEX:	1.61 to 1.63
CRYSTAL SYSTEM:	monoclinic, aggregate
SPECIFIC GRAVITY:	2.95
MOHS HARDNESS:	6 to 6.5
VISUAL IDENTIFYING CHARACTERISTICS:	rough fractures with a dull lustre

INSTRUCTIONS FOR INSTALLATION OF EMERALD OR GREEN JADE

Emeralds or green jade would best be purchased, as well as set, on a Wednesday and when Mercury is in its own sign or nakshatra (if possible), as previously delineated, or a friendly sign or nakshatra. The weight of emerald should be no less than 1 carat, but 2 carats is better. Jade should be at least 5 carats in weight. It may be set in yellow or white gold, silver, or platinum, but yellow gold is optimum. If worn as a ring it is placed on the smallest finger, preferably on the right hand. Whether a ring or pendant, it must be open-backed and set so that the stone comes into contact with the skin. For more empowerment the following ritual may be performed on a Wednesday, two hours after Sunrise:

1) rinse emerald or jade ring/pendant in water

2) rinse in cow's milk

3) rinse again in water

4) place on altar/shrine, or in a sacred place before a picture of the presiding deity of Mercury, or a Mercury Yantra

5) light incense

6) meditate on desired benefits

7) repeat mantra 108 times: *"Om Bum Budhaya Namah Om"*

8) place on small finger, or on chain around neck

YELLOW SAPPHIRE - GEMSTONE OF JUPITER

THE PLANET JUPITER

Jupiter, by nature, is the most wonderful and expansive planet giving to the human race their most munificent qualities. It is the most pious of planets, known as guru or teacher. A strong Jupiter will be found in the horoscopes of wealthy and influential persons. Jupiter is the signifier of good luck and good fortune, as well as being indicative of long distance travel We understand the good karma earned in the previous lives by the placement of Jupiter.

Jupiter is also the ruler of religion and religious devotions and thus comes the name, Guru. He is the controller of all other planets, the revered spiritual master of the demigods. Philosophy and spirituality are under the auspices of Jupiter, as are financial affairs and wealth. Jupiter is also the indicator of children in the chart and, in a woman's horoscope, it is the indicator of what kind of a husband she will attain in this life and what their relationship will be like.   A strong Jupiter indicates one whose opinions are valued by many, therefore teachers fall in this category. Jupiter is noble, dignified, optimistic, of good humour and the giver of the fruits of labour.

Jupiter is ruler of the zodiacal signs Sagittarius and Pisces, is exalted in Cancer and debilitated in Capricorn. He gives especially beneficial effects posited in the nakshatras of Uttara Phalguni, Uttarashadha, Punarvasu, Purvabhadrapad and Vishaka. Jupiter has a .friendly relationship with the Sun, Moon, and Mars. Saturn, Rahu, and Ketu are neutral to him, but Mercury and Venus are his enemies.

A strong or well-placed Jupiter can indicate many things, all of them positive, giving happiness. Subjects will be of an optimistic frame of mind, have dignity and a good sense of humour. It can make a person famous and gives many good qualities, such as honesty, compassion towards others, and wisdom. Although a powerful Jupiter may give much wealth or influence, more importantly it makes for a happy and satisfied life. What riches can equal the contentment of a mind at rest with the accomplishments of life?

Those with a well-placed Jupiter in their chart are generally religious, philosophical and try to live a fairly pious life. They will engage in spiritual meditation and inquire as to the true purpose of human life in this world. This is the greatest boon. To attempt to uncover the true "self", to become "self-realised" is the ultimate goal of life. Those who engage in actions designed to remove the covering of "maya" (illusion or "that which is not") are understood to be of the highest calibre of human beings. The Vedas consider that the person who tries to solve the problem of repeated birth and death in the material world, transmigrating through 8,400,000 species of life, is of the most developed intelligence and greatly fortunate. The Vedic philosophy of karma is that a soul gets the reactions to his past actions, so a well-placed Jupiter indicates one who has been of a pious nature in previous lives. "As one sows, so he shall reap"; this is the immutable law of action and reaction.

Well-placed Jupiter gives compassion, benevolence, charity, morality, wisdom and truthfulness. Anyone with great ambition is influenced by Jupiter, as are priests, monks and spiritual teachers. He rules those in political and legal professions and those who have control over their external senses. Physically Jupiter rules the blood circulation in our arteries, the liver, thighs and "fat" in the body.

When Jupiter is weak in the horoscope subjects may suffer from lack of happiness and enthusiasm. They will be weak-willed, have a lack of faith, both spiritually and in the good things and attributes of life. Life may seem meaningless and without a source of pleasure. A weak Jupiter will cause pessimism and depression, anxiety and self-pity. Ill-aspected Jupiter makes for a lack of compassion and congeniality for other people. It will also give rise to material, as well as financial, difficulties. The person may be devoid of any creative abilities and, in the case of a woman, may be unable to bear children and lack a good husband to properly care for her.

Physically, there may be a weak immune system and generally poor vitality. The body weight may be too low and the liver and pancreas may not function properly. It can give rise to problems like arthritis or jaundice and disease of the respiratory system. An appearance of general physical debility is not uncommon when Jupiter is badly afflicted.

YELLOW SAPPHIRE

Yellow sapphire is the gemstone recommended to be worn for a weak Jupiter. The yellow sapphire will radiate the qualities of generosity, wisdom and compassion. It serves to strengthen the Jupiterian energy and attract the energies ruled over by Jupiter. Many times a change is effected in financial status within a short period of time. It serves to bring material abundance and prosperity, as well as a more philosophical outlook on life. Those that practice meditation find that in wearing the yellow sapphire, their ability to concentrate increases, thereby magnifying the peace and joy reaped from such spiritual discipline. Physically , it can raise levels of energy, help to gain needed body weight and to strengthen the overall immune system.

Yellow sapphires should be flawless to the eye and of a lemony-yellow colour. It is commonly heat-treated to make it more saleable to the public, although many people have never seen nor heard of one. If heated it gets a darker golden, or brownish yellow colour and this material is useless for our purposes, for its inherent potencies have been destroyed in the heating process.

It is to be set in rings or pendants of yellow gold and, if in a ring, is best worn on the forefinger (next to the thumb) of the right hand. It may also be worn on the ring finger of the right hand.

There are several sources of yellow sapphires including Sri Lanka, Thailand, Cambodia, Burma, Australia and Africa, but the only place I seem to be able to still purchase enough natural (unheated) material is Sri Lanka, or India (where the stones originate from Sri Lanka).

Yellow topaz may be substituted for yellow sapphire and its effects are thought to be almost as potent. Citrine quartz may also be substituted for yellow sapphire, although its potencies are less. The important thing is to take advantage of the powers of gems according to your own means. If worn properly, with faith and determination, achievement of the desired effects will come about quickly.

Gemological Characteristics of Yellow Sapphire

SPECIES:	Corundum
TRANSPARENCY:	Transparent
COLOUR:	Yellow, golden, and various lighter and darker shades with mixtures of brown or orange
REFRACTIVE INDEX:	1.762 to 1.77
BIREFRINGENCE:	0.008
PLEOCHROISM:	Strong dichroism
CRYSTAL SYSTEM:	Hexagonal
OPTIC CHARACTER:	Doubly refractive
SPECIFIC GRAVITY:	4.0
MOHS HARDNESS:	9
DISPERSION:	0.018
FLUORESCENCE:	none for yellow sapphire
VISUAL IDENTIFYING CHARACTERISTICS:	Hexagonal growth lines, fingerprint inclusions, rutile (silk) needles, straight colour banding

Instructions for Installation of Yellow Sapphire

A yellow sapphire would ideally be purchased on a Thursday, when the Moon is waxing and in the nakshatra of Pushya (best), Punarvasu, Vishaka, or Purvabhadrapada. The weight should be at least 2 carats and it must be mounted in yellow gold.

Once the proper gem has been acquired, whether mounted in a ring or pendant, the back must be open so that the gemstone comes into contact with the skin. A ring is best worn on the Jupiter finger (forefinger) of the right hand, but may be worn on the Sun finger (ring finger). For further empowerment the following short ritual may be performed on a Thursday, one hour before Sunset:

1) rinse yellow sapphire ring/pendant with water

2) rinse in cow's milk

3) rinse again in water

4) place ring/pendant on home altar/shrine (or sacred place) before a picture of Brihaspati (the ruler of Jupiter) or a Jupiter Yantra

5) light incense

6) meditate on desired benefits

7) chant mantra and repeat 108 times: *"Om Brim Brihaspataye Namah Om"*

8) place ring on forefinger of right hand or pendant on chain around the neck

DIAMOND - GEMSTONE OF VENUS

THE PLANET VENUS

Venus is a benefic planet by nature and is also considered to be a teacher. Venus is the planet governing sensuality and is the embodiment of love. All attributes of love, romance, beauty, sensuality, sexual pleasures and passion are under the rule of Venus.

The sanskrit name for Venus is "Shukra", which in one instance means "semen", making Venus the presiding deity of semen. Shukra is the son of the great sage, seer and astrologer "Bhrigu", who taught his son all spiritual sciences and the vedic scriptures.

Venus is also very important in determining wealth and conjugal relationships. It represents marriage and the ability to gain a good wife. The comforts of having luxuries, a comfortable home, quality cars, furniture, and paraphernalia are also under Venus' control. Like Jupiter, Venus also gives wealth and material prosperity, but Venus often concentrates on the material rather than the spiritual attributes, unless the subject has the ability to utilise its "higher" aspects.

Venus is connected to the chanting of mantras, Tantra, hypnotism, alchemy and the medical arts. Venus rules artists, actors, musicians, dancers and poets. Those that make a living dealing in the sensual things available on earth also usually have a strong, or prominent Venus in their horoscopes.

In the physical body it rules the reproductive system, kidneys, eyes, cheeks, chin and throat. In nature it especially rules over flowers, jewels and tropical places. Venus is lord of the signs Taurus and Libra.

It is exalted in Pisces, and debilitated in Virgo. Nakshatras ruled by Venus are Bharani, Purvaphalguni and Purvashadha. Friends are Mercury and Saturn, Sun and Moon are enemies and Mars and Jupiter are neutral, although Venus is hostile towards Jupiter.

When Venus is strong in the chart , subjects may be loving and charismatic, able to infuse others with a sense of happiness and well-being. It brings wealth, comforts and a beautiful face and body. It makes for mutual attraction to the opposite sex. Venus may bestow a gentle and tender nature, having great consideration for others around them. It gives an affinity for fine jewellery, beautiful clothes, ornaments and perfumes. Those with a prominent Venus will usually enjoy both rich and flavourful foods and have a love for the fine arts. They may have the inspiration necessary to become artists, musicians, or poets. Hopefully they may also be seekers of truth and the knowledge of little-known, or secret, sciences. Qualities of expression, appreciation and affection are apparent in those with a well-positioned Venus.

If Venus is weak or afflicted in the horoscope, problems in marriage often result. Subjects may be lacking in physical beauty, as well as grace and charm. Insensitivity may be seen along with a lack of love and affection. A weak Venus can result in coarse and vulgar behaviour. Romantic affairs will be seen to be tumultuous and short-lived. There appears to be a difficulty in expressing feelings. In men, relationships with women are extremely difficult and, in women, it may be seen to bring about a lack of feminine qualities.

Physically, it may cause weak kidneys and reproductive system, or even infertility. Energy may be low and the immune system may also be feeble. Chronic urinary tract infections may also be manifest. Even if Venus is strong, if it is in an undesirable position, it may cause an overindulgence in sex, eating, or drinking, bringing on innumerable physical inebrieties.

DIAMOND

Diamond is the gemstone recommended for a weak Venus. It increases artistic and creative abilities. It can also lead toward love and devotion in relationships. It may also increase passion and sexual desires, especially in women and can be good for marriage.

Physically, it can strengthen the reproductive system, and is said to aid in the treatment of chronic diseases. Diamonds also increase affinities for a luxurious and indulgent lifestyle. Anyone already living such a life should be careful not to increase this energy too much, for overindulgence can be a cause of disease and dissatisfaction. White, or colourless sapphire, is also a substitute for diamond, as is natural turquoise and may be used in the same manner as diamond.

Major sources of diamonds are Africa (many countries there are producers), Australia, Russia, India, Indonesia, Venezuela, Brazil and Guyana. There are no synthetic diamonds on the commercial market at present, basically because of the high cost of production. It has been a fear of gemologists world-wide that someday it may become cost-effective. This is because, to date, there is no absolutely foolproof way of discerning a natural diamond from the synthetic. Most synthetics produced are practically flawless, giving no identifying characteristics to make them distinguishable.

There are many diamond substitutes, from colourless gems like white sapphire or white spinel, to others like cubic zirconium which has great brilliance and scintillation like diamond. However, any gemologist can easily tell the difference. There is a fairly new treatment, invented in Israel, which fills the fractures in a diamond so well that it's almost impossible to tell. The process is a guarded secret but so far I know of no instances where this treatment has been used, but not disclosed to the customer.

Individuals should be careful of wearing a diamond that has any discoloration, dark flaws, or fractures of any type. If a diamond with such imperfections is worn it will cause havoc in a person's life, rather than the beneficial influences being sought. It is much better to obtain a colourless sapphire, other colourless faceted gemstone, or natural turquoise, to enhance the positive energies of Venus. They are affordable and give good effect. Diamonds should weigh at least 1 carat, but 1.5 to 2 is better. Substitute stones in faceted colourless gems, such as white sapphire, should be at least 2-3 carats and turquoise at least 5 carats.

GEMOLOGICAL CHARACTERISTICS OF DIAMOND

SPECIES:	Diamond
TRANSPARENCY:	Transparent
COLOUR:	Colourless, yellow, pink, blue, red, brown, black
REFRACTIVE INDEX:	2.417
CRYSTAL SYSTEM:	Cubic
OPTIC CHARACTER:	Singly refractive
SPECIFIC GRAVITY:	3.52
MOHS HARDNESS:	10 (hardest substance known to man)
DISPERSION:	0.044
FLUORESCENCE:	Inert to strong blue-white under long or short wave
VISUAL IDENTIFYING CHARACTERISTICS:	Sharp facet edges, waxy to rough girdle, adamantine lustre, naturals, cleavage

INSTRUCTIONS FOR INSTALLATION OF DIAMOND

A diamond should be purchased on a Friday, preferably when Venus is in its own or exalted sign, or in an auspicious nakshatra (as mentioned in the text about Venus). Give consideration to at least a carat, or only slightly less, although 1.5 to 2 carats is preferable.

It is advisable to be set in a white metal which may be either silver, platinum, or white gold and the mounting (ring or pendant) must have an open back, so that the stone comes into direct contact with the skin. It is best worn on the middle or small fingers of either hand, although diamond may also be worn on the "ring finger", as it is used for engagement and wedding rings. For more empowerment the following short ritual may be performed on a Friday, at Sunrise:

1) rinse diamond ring/pendant in water

2) rinse in cow's milk

3) rinse again with water

4) place on home altar/shrine (or a sacred place in the home) before a picture of Shukracarya (the presiding deity of Venus) or a Venus Yantra

5) light incense

6) meditate on desired benefits

7) chant mantra and repeat 108 times: *"Om Shum Shukraya Namah Om"*

8) place ring on middle, smallest, or ring finger of either hand, or if pendant on chain around neck

Blue Sapphire - Gemstone of Saturn

The Planet Saturn

Saturn is a slow-moving and very powerful planet, malefic in nature. Shani is the Sanskrit name for Saturn and he is also called Shanaishchara (slow moving) as Saturn takes 2.5 years, or 30 months, to pass through all signs of the zodiac. It is the ruler of longevity of life, death and the ageing of the body. It controls the practice of yoga and renunciation, or detachment, from this material world. Therefore, it rules over ascetics, monks and spiritual renunciates. It also indicates foreigners and foreign lands in the chart. Saturn is also the ruler of people dealing in the black market, as well as thieves and robbers.

Said to be the greatest teacher, Saturn is a hard task-master. The lessons learned should help a subject to gain a spiritual perspective on life and the realisation that full satisfaction can never be possible while transmigrating from one birth to another within this material world.

Coincidentally transport, machinery and prisons are also ruled by Saturn and, in a way, this whole material stratosphere of innumerable planets, planetary systems and forced birth and death is viewed as a large prison. The reason this allegory is used in the vedas to describe the material planetary systems is that we are not truly "free" until liberated from its confines. This can only happen when man becomes self-realised and renounces the temporary pleasures (and pains) of this world.

Manual labourers are especially represented by Saturn, but its position in everyone's horoscope will indicate the type of employment in which they engage. This may also be interpreted as indicating the trials and tribulations to be gone through to attain success in the chosen field.

Saturn rules over carpenters and construction workers, labourers, mechanics, miners, masons, vendors, hunters and social servants. Saturn also rules over products such as gasoline, iron, wood and all black-coloured items. Deadly substances also come under Saturn's direction.

Saturn is lord of the signs Capricorn and Aquarius. He is exalted in Libra and debilitated in Aries. His friends are Mercury, Venus, Rahu and Ketu. Enemies are Sun, Moon and Mars. Jupiter is neutral. He is ruler of the nakshatras Pushya, Anuradha and Uttarabhadrapada. Saturn is most powerful during the waning of the Moon and shows its greatest effect between the ages of 36 and 42 years. Physically Saturn rules the bones, nails, teeth, and hair. He also has to do with the nervous system, as he will give a body constitution dominated by "vata" (air or wind) and nerve impulses are related with the element of air. It is also an indicator of psychological problems.

If Saturn is well-positioned, or aspected, in the horoscope, it gives long life, the ability to be a leader and an organiser with integrity, sincerity and honesty. If well positioned, it can also give wisdom, fame and patience, along with a sense of justice, or knowing right from wrong. It can help spiritualists become unattached for advancement in their spiritual goals.

When Saturn is in a poor position it brings disappointments, sorrow and miseries. It may cause delays and difficulties, disputes and disharmony. It may cause subjects to feel despondent or dejected, and cause destruction or death. A weak position can cause enmity, theft, lawsuits and imprisonment. Accidents and premature ageing are also possible effects of a poorly positioned Saturn, which can make its subordinates lonely, sadistic, greedy and afraid. Dishonesty, irresponsibility and addiction to drugs are also traits of those with a poorly positioned Saturn. These people may be agitated and unable to handle stress. They are not practical and have a warped perception of reality. Some may suffer problems from the government and have a hard time earning a living. They give up easily and have no endurance or drive, over a long period of time.

Physically, there may be weakness of nerves and the bones, lack of vitality, and a short life. Ear disease or deafness , gout, colic and asthma may also be caused by the malefic influence of Saturn. Resistance to infectious diseases may be extremely weak and, in severe cases, cancer, epilepsy, paralysis and severe mental debility, or insanity, may manifest.

BLUE SAPPHIRE

Blue sapphire is the gemstone recommended to strengthen Saturn. It can be beneficial to career or work and promote feelings of self-contentment or detachment. It is also said to counteract envy and give protection while travelling and from mental anxieties. It can also help to counteract misfortunes brought on by a poorly positioned Saturn in the horoscope.

Physically, it is said to strengthen the bones and cleanse the blood. Spiritually, it is an aid in meditation and it increases psychic abilities.

Blue sapphires are mainly heat-treated today to improve their intensity of colour, as well as to melt certain "silk" inclusions to make them disappear from vision. It's important to know the gem you purchase is natural, not a common synthetic, and free from treatment with heat, or any other so-called "enhancements". Gems which have been heated have no potency. The electromagnetic energy inherent in the stone is destroyed by this process. They are useless other than for adorning the body, or getting some benefit through the blue colour alone.

A light coloured stone can have good effects, but an over-dark stone will not. They even look "dead" to the eye and mostly these are heated stones, anyway. Again, as with all other gems, if you are not expert in gemology yourself, be sure you know that the person you purchase from is expert and is reputable. I have seen many blue sapphires that have been sold as natural, but it is obvious that they are heated.

The best sources for natural, unheated sapphires are Sri Lanka and India, but again, "BUYERS BEWARE!" —Don't buy gems from source countries without the expertise. You're bound to get cheated. Other sources for blue sapphires are Burma, Thailand, Cambodia, U.S. (Montana), and Australia. Kashmir is also a source of the finest and most expensive blue sapphires in the world, but they are extremely rare nowadays.

GEMOLOGICAL CHARACTERISTICS OF BLUE SAPPHIRE

SPECIES:	Corundum
TRANSPARENCY:	Transparent to translucent (latter mostly cut"en cabachon" (dome shaped with flat bottom)
COLOUR:	Blue, purple/violet, and mixtures of shades of blue with purple, grey, black, or green
REFRACTIVE INDEX:	1.762 to 1.77
BIREFRINGENCE:	0.008
PLEOCHROISM:	Strong dichroism
CRYSTAL SYSTEM:	Hexagonal
OPTIC CHARACTER:	Doubly refractive
SPECIFIC GRAVITY:	4
MOHS HARDNESS:	9
DISPERSION:	0.018
FLUORESCENCE:	Lighter coloured blue sapphires under long wave show moderate to strong pink. Purple coloured sapphires are inert to strong reddish-purple under long wave and inert to medium red under short wave
VISUAL IDENTIFYING CHARACTERISTICS:	Hexagonal growth lines, fingerprint inclusions, rutile (silk) needles, straight colour banding

INSTRUCTIONS FOR INSTALLATION OF BLUE SAPPHIRE

Blue sapphire should be purchased on a Saturday, if possible when Saturn is in its own sign or exalted sign, or own or friendly nakshatra. The gem must weigh at least 2 carats, and ideally be free from flaws and imperfections, especially any black inclusions. The ring or pendant is best set in a mounting made of a mixture of gold, iron and silver, but gold, silver, or platinum may be used. Amethyst or lapis-lazuli may be substituted for blue sapphire, but their weights should be between 5 and 10 carats as their vibrations are somewhat weaker than blue sapphire.

For more empowerment the following short ritual may be used on a Saturday, 2 and a half hours before Sunset:

1) rinse blue sapphire ring/pendant in water

2) rinse in cow's milk

3) rinse again in water

4) place on altar/shrine (or sacred place in home) before a picture of the predominating deity of Saturn, or Saturn Yantra

5) light incense

6) meditate on desired benefits

7) chant mantra, repeating 108 times, as follows: *"Om Sham Shanaishcharaya Namah Om"*

8) place ring on middle finger of right hand or, if in a pendant, place on chain and around the neck

ON RAHU AND KETU

A NOTE ON THE FOLLOWING TWO SECTIONS

Rahu and Ketu are known as the north node of the moon, (or dragon's head) and the south node of the moon, (or dragon's tail,) respectively. These nodes were not mentioned in the very oldest vedic astrological references. Only the seven major planets are spoken of in the most ancient scriptures' texts on astronomy and astrology. We first hear of them in the "Mahabharata" in a story which I will relate here.

This story takes place on another planet, called Dhruvaloka. This planet is said to be the only planet within this material sphere which is not annihilated at the time of dissolution, when the universes are being sucked back to whence they came. The modern scientists also believe this will happen, but what they don't understand is that it is being done fully under the control of the Supreme Personality of Godhead, Maha-Vishnu. This planet is where it is said that the demigods, which include planetary deities, approach Lord Vishnu within this material sphere. On Dhruvaloka there is an ocean of milk.

Actually there are different types of oceans existing on different planets within the different planetary systems. We have oceans of salt water, but there are also oceans of fresh water existing on some planets, oceans of oil on others (why should this be any more fantastic than our having lakes of oil underground in places on earth?) and oceans of other liquid substances, as well. In the ocean of milk is an island called "Svetadvipa" where Lord Vishnu resides. The demigods come here from their various planets when they desire the favour of Vishnu, for they are all His devotees.

We always read the stories of the struggles between the demigods and the antigods (those of demoniac mentality called "danavas"), the ongoing struggle between the forces of good and evil, which appear in many stories within the scriptures. According to the ancient references, both the demigods and danavas were sons of the great sage and mystic "Kasyapa Muni", but born of different wives. The demigods were always religious and spiritually cognisant of the higher purpose of existence, whilst the danavas were only interested in their material wealth and how to enjoy God's bounties, but without any recognition of their source.

At times the danavas would gain certain advances such that they would cause great disturbances to all other living entities on other planets. Such is the nature of this type of mentality. (It is always existing and certainly we see it on our planet in abundance, so disturbing to any sane, spiritually directed person.)

As this story goes the demigods wished to obtain an ambrosia or "nectar of immortality" which was only to be found in the depths of the milk ocean. It could only be obtained by churning the waters of the milk ocean, which the demigods could not do alone. For this they needed the help of the danavas, who were only too willing, desiring this nectar of immortality for themselves. They agreed to help the demigods for a portion of the nectar, which was agreed. The churning rod used was a mountain of the name "Mandara" and the ropes to churn it were formed by the body of the serpent "Vasuki". Lord Vishnu assumed the form of a giant tortoise and His shell became the pivot for churning the mountain to produce the nectar. The demigods and danavas churned the ocean and the nectar was produced.

Lord Vishnu then assumed the form of the most beautiful woman, Mohini, of a beauty far beyond our imagination. She kept the nectar in a pot and said She would distribute it, but that the demigods and danavas must sit in two separate rows.

Being fully captivated by Mohini's beauty, the danavas agreed and sat separately from the demigods. Mohini began to distribute the nectar. Rahu, one of the danavas, saw that the danavas were being fooled into thinking they were getting nectar, but the fact was that the demigods were getting the nectar and the danavas were being given "varuni" (a liquor).

None of the other danavas noticed. Rahu decided to fool the demigods by dressing himself as a demigod and sitting within their midst. Accordingly he was given the nectar to drink. However, before the nectar passed down Rahu's throat into his body, "Surya", the demigod of the Sun planet and "Chandra", demigod of the Moon, realised the deception. They immediately informed Lord Vishnu and the assembly of demigods.

Instantly Lord Vishnu cut Rahu's head from his body with His "Disc" and threw it into the sky. The trunk fell to the earth, but was also immortal, having already had a share of the nectar. Both parts of the danava Rahu were put into orbit 180° from each other, so that they could never join together. The trunk of Rahu's body became Ketu.

As Surya (Sun) and Chandra (Moon) were the demigods who found out Rahu's deception, Rahu and Ketu became their greatest enemies. It is said that this inimical relationship goes on, and that when there is a solar or lunar eclipse, it is Rahu or Ketu causing it by trying to swallow the luminaries. Being without body they escape through Rahu's neck and with Ketu being headless, they also escape through his neck.

Comets and meteors are said to be born of Ketu.

When Sun, Moon, and the nodes line up at the same zodiacal longitude, an eclipse happens. Due to the fact that the speed at which the planets and luminaries move is constant, eclipses of the Sun and Moon can be calculated and foretold many hundreds of years before they are due to take place, giving them great importance for those in the astronomical and astrological fields.

Not being actual luminaries Rahu and Ketu are considered "shadow planets". Being the north and south nodes of the Moon, they become representative of the bipolarity of cosmic energy, the cosmos being the macrocosm and the individual souls the microcosm. Most astrological texts say they do not cast aspects, nor own any zodiacal sign. However, they do have signs of exaltation and debilitation and are stronger in some signs than others. (They are the rulers, though, of certain nakshatras, or constellations.) Both of these planets are malefic by nature and, to a great degree, represent the particular mentality developed in the last life. Often they are referred to as "karmic indicators" or "karmic control planets".

In every horoscope cast they are present, bisecting the natal chart. Generally it is said that Rahu will act like Saturn and Ketu like Mars. They also take on the attributes of the planet ruling the sign in which they are posited.

HESSONITE - GEMSTONE OF RAHU

THE PLANET RAHU

Rahu is a malefic planet by nature. It brings chaos generally, causing difficulties, frustration, anxiety and suffering. It can cause ignorance, enmity and insatiable sensual or worldly desires, robbing those so influenced of the ability to ever feel satisfied. It can indicate infectious disease, unclean or irreligious habits and use of intoxicants. It generally intensifies the effects of any house in which it is situated.

Rahu represents snakes, fear, suffering from sinful actions and persons of lower character. It rules over travellers and navigators, as well as criminals, spies, anarchists, revolutionaries and terrorists. Persons of violent and aggressive natures are also ruled by Rahu. It causes people to go underground, losing contact with people they previously associated with in life.

When situated in a powerful position, Rahu can give great riches, or the ability to use the media to sway the opinions of the public. It can give power and fame, political success, as well as physical beauty. However, Rahu's planetary period will never allow a person to feel satisfied, regardless of any material gains. Whatever is gained in Rahu's period is also usually lost. He shows his full effects between the ages of 42 and 48 years.

Rahu is said to be exalted in Taurus in most references, but some give Gemini or Virgo as the exaltation sign. Nevertheless it is powerful in any of these signs. Mercury, Saturn and Venus are friendly to Rahu, but Mars, Sun and Moon are his enemies. Jupiter is neutral. Rahu is especially powerful in giving artistic and communicative talents, or knowledge of mystical arts when conjunct with Jupiter or Venus.

When badly positioned, Rahu makes for poor judgement. Those so influenced are usually illogical, insensitive and selfish. It can cause fears and suicidal tendencies. Hallucinations and taking of drugs are some of the effects of Rahu, which in turn lead to moodiness, fantasies, or imagined problems. Rahu can even induce a person to commit murder. Those powerfully under his rays can be swayed by any influences, regardless of the dangers and are usually unpopular, with very few friends. They are generally self destructive and easily lose control of themselves, often ending up in detention or prison.

Physically, Rahu can cause a weak immune system, thereby contracting diseases easily. Subjects are nervous, with an unhealthy pallor to their appearance. Disorders include constipation or dysentery, rheumatism, skin diseases, cholera and piles, to name but a few, together with many diseases difficult or impossible to diagnose easily. People so influenced may lose control of bodily functions and steadily degenerate with nervous and mental disorders.

HESSONITE

Hessonite is the gemstone recommended for strengthening Rahu. It is a type of garnet. In better qualities it is of a reddish-orange-honey colour. It is called "gomedak" in sanskrit, or "gomed" in Hindi, the language understood by most people living in India.

The use of this stone increases creativity and good use of the imagination. It may also serve to increase the level of self confidence and reduce the propensity to be fearful. It can also increase the awareness of a person's subtle senses and increase ambition, which may also be for spiritual advancement.

Physically, it is said to help nervous disorders and such degenerative diseases as cancer, of which Rahu can be the cause. It may improve immune functions and counteract the harmful effects of radiation. Hessonite is said to help avert disasters and to protect against evil spirits. Supposedly it can prevent or avert insanity and protect from sudden misfortunes. It also has a reputation for giving great abilities in the sciences.

The source countries are Africa, Burma and Sri Lanka. As Hessonite is a type of grossularite garnet, any other type of golden grossularite garnet may be used as a substitute.

GEMOLOGICAL CHARACTERISTICS OF HESSONITE

SPECIES: Grossularite

TRANSPARENCY: Transparent

COLOUR:	Golden-orange with tints of brown or red
REFRACTIVE INDEX:	1.74 to 1.75
CRYSTAL SYSTEM:	Cubic
OPTIC CHARACTER:	Singly refractive
SPECIFIC GRAVITY:	3.61
MOHS HARDNESS:	7
DISPERSION:	0.028
FLUORESCENCE:	Inert
VISUAL IDENTIFYING CHARACTERISTICS:	Typical garnet inclusions, "roiled" or"heat-wave" effect, anomalous double-refraction, strain colours

INSTRUCTIONS FOR INSTALLATION OF HESSONITE

A hessonite should be purchased on a Saturday, when the Moon is in the nakshatras of Ardra, Swati, or Satabisha and when the Moon is waxing. It must weigh a minimum of 2 carats, with 3 or more being optimum. It is best set in a combination of gold, iron and silver metals, but any of them, as well as platinum, may be used. As usual the mounting, whether ring or pendant, must have an open back to allow the gemstone to come into contact with the wearer's skin. If in a ring, it is to be worn on either the middle or smallest finger of the left hand.

For more empowerment the following short ritual may be followed on a Saturday, 2 hours after Sunset:

1) rinse hessonite ring/pendant in water

2) rinse in cow's milk

3) rinse again in water

4) place on home altar/shrine (or in a sacred place) before a picture of Rahu, or a Rahu Yantra

5) light incense

6) meditate on desired benefits

7) chant mantra 108 times: *"Om Ram Rahuve Namah Om"*

8) place ring on middle or small finger of left hand, or as a pendant on chain around the neck

CAT'S EYE - GEMSTONE OF KETU

THE PLANET KETU

Ketu, like Rahu, is a shadow planet and again is malefic by nature. It is actually a spiritual planet and an indicator of enlightenment. It gives spiritual tendencies and nonattachment to material ambition or worldly desires. It can give the wisdom to attain spiritual knowledge, or knowledge of the self (self-realisation). Accordingly it is considered a "moksha-karaka", or a force which can lead to enlightenment and freedom from the cycle of repeated birth and death.

To those so influenced it may give psychic potencies, giving them great abilities in the healing arts. Subjects may become adept in natural forms of healing body and mind, herbology, tantra and the way of dealing with those disturbed by forces on the astral plane. This may include ghosts and other malefic spirits. Ketu may also cause such severe physical illness in the body that, as a positive consequence, subjects become disinterested in material life and seek spiritual liberation.

Ketu is exalted in Scorpio (or as with Rahu some consider both Mercury's signs Gemini and Virgo to be exaltation), is debilitated in Taurus and is strong in either of Jupiter's signs of Sagittarius or Pisces, as well as (clearly) the signs of Mercury. He rules the nakshatras of Ashvini, Magha and Mula.

One rule is that if Rahu is somehow favouring a person, then Ketu will be unfavourable. Ketu is basically a restrictive planet, in one way or another. He afflicts the body as Rahu afflicts mind. His position may indicate things concerning hands and feet, the mother relationship and shows its greatest effects between the ages of 48 and 54 years.

Ketu can force an impoverished material situation and generally afflicts whatever house in which it is positioned within the horoscope. When afflicted it can cause fear, anxiety, accidents and imprisonment. It can cause destruction in strange and terrible ways, starvation and even death. Poisons also come under Ketu's control. It may make people conspire to do terrible things and may give nightmares to those so influenced. Materially, Ketu is generally thought of as causing suffering.

When Ketu is poorly placed in the chart, a subject will have weak eyesight and concentration, be indiscriminate and lack confidence. They may be extremely accident-prone, or have self-destructive tendencies. Some will feel constricted without the freedom to do as they might like. A tendency to dwell on the past, or worry about things that are already beyond reparation may also manifest, and it can cause nightmares. When conjunct with another planet, it causes the planet to act in an erratic way, reducing or destroying its potency and the categories of the house in which it is situated.

Physically, it may cause the circulation to be poor, bad digestion, anaemia, ulcers, too much heat within the body and muscular or nervous system disorders. It is also the cause of terribly disfiguring skin diseases, such as leprosy. Additionally, it is a cause of pains and disease in the joints and nerves. Like Rahu, it can cause strange diseases that may be difficult to diagnose, as well as incurable problems like cancer or paralysis.

Cat's-Eye

Cat's-Eye is the gemstone recommended for Ketu; specifically Chrysoberyl cat's-eye. The finest quality is called "milk and honey", as the stone is a honey colour, with the eye white, like milk. The darker varieties are generally a greenish body colour. Dark, especially black imperfections should be strictly avoided in this stone (as with most others) as wearing such a stone can cause early demise. The source countries for cat's-eyes are India, Burma, Sri Lanka and Brazil.

Cat's-Eye is said to increase powers of perception and insight. It should also give greater discrimination of action. The ancients believed that cat's-eye protected individuals from epidemics or diseases, from drowning and from enemies, as well as heightening psychic perceptions. Coincidentally it is supposed to bring good fortune to gamblers. Apatite cat's-eye or any other variety of cat's-eye may be substituted for cat's-eye Chrysoberyl.

Gemological Characteristics of Cat's-Eye

SPECIES:	Chrysoberyl
TRANSPARENCY:	Transparent to translucent
COLOUR:	Golden-yellow, greenish-yellow, golden or yellowish-brown, reddish-brown, black, white and grey

REFRACTIVE INDEX:	1.746 to 1.755
BIREFRINGENCE:	0.009
PLEOCHROISM:	Weak to strong dichroism or trichroism
CRYSTAL SYSTEM:	Orthorhombic
OPTIC CHARACTER:	Doubly refractive
SPECIFIC GRAVITY:	3.73
MOHS HARDNESS:	8.5
DISPERSION:	0.015
FLUORESCENCE:	Inert
VISUAL IDENTIFYING CHARACTERISTICS:	Chatoyancy (causes the phenomenon of the eye), fingerprint inclusions

INSTRUCTIONS FOR INSTALLATION OF CAT'S-EYE

Cat's-eye is ideally purchased on a Wednesday, Thursday, or Friday when the Moon is in the signs of Sagittarius, Pisces, or Aries, or in the constellations (nakshatras) of Ashvini, Mula, or Magha. It should be at least 3 carats and of a good colour, free of harmful imperfections. It may be set in a combination of gold, iron and silver or, alternatively, in one of them, or platinum. The normal rule that it is mounted in a ring or pendant with an open back to allow the gem to contact the wearer's skin applies and, if a ring, is worn on the small finger of the left hand.

For more empowerment the following short ritual may be performed on a Thursday, any time between two hours after sunset to midnight:

1) rinse cat's-eye ring/pendant in water

2) rinse in cow's milk

3) rinse again in water

4) place on home altar/shrine (or sacred place) before a picture of Ketu, or a Ketu Yantra

5) light incense

6) meditate on desired benefits

7) chant mantra 108 times: *"Om Kaim Ketave Namah Om"*

8) place ring on small finger of left hand, or pendant on chain and around the neck

CONCLUSION

The healing powers of using mantras, yantras and gemstones cannot be underestimated. The sacred sound vibrations of the vedic mantras are meant to purify the body, mind and spirit to allow the practitioner to rise above the mundane material consciousness of dwelling upon temporary matter.

Yantras are a powerful tool for worship of the Divine and for directing consciousness toward higher dimensional planes of existence. Very little bona-fide information has been available to the English-speaking public on this subject and I hope this work goes some way to rectifying that situation.

The system of gemstone therapy has been widely used by vedic astrologers, tantrics and ayurvedic doctors for thousands of years, with beneficial results being gained in most cases.

It was also used widely by the Greeks in their system of medicine, known in India as the "unani system". Both of these systems (ayurveda and unani) understand the elements and humours of the body. They understand the causes of imbalances within the human organism and how to help the body's natural ability to heal itself, thereby overcoming these imbalances. Gems are elemental forms of energy in pure crystalline form and, as our bodies are ultimately composed of these same substances, so the use of gemstone therapy is a natural and extremely effective way of healing on the physical, as well as emotional level.

Vedic astrology recommends the uses of mantras, yantras and gems as a "healing" or "remedial" measure to help attain optimum physical and mental health. Only in such a pure state can we understand our true constitution as spirit. Our nature is spiritual energy, individually as spirit souls. We inhabit these physical bodies for a short time only in each lifetime.

Vedic astrology is also called "Jyotish", or the "science of light". It is said in the vedas that "knowledge is light and ignorance is darkness".

When one is in ignorance of the world within and without, then there is fear. If there is real knowledge, then there is no fear, not of any circumstance in life, nor of the inevitable death of the body. Therefore, the holy sciences of astrology and ayurveda are meant to help us advance toward cosmic consciousness, rather than exclusively deal with the temporary bodies and mental conditions related only to this present bodily form.

Our external goals and desires of this life need to be fulfilled, but in a way which is in harmony with "reality". The vedic system is meant to help a person achieve these goals, but in a way that leads to the ultimate goal of life, namely liberation from material consciousness.

Astrology is there to give knowledge of this life that we may be forewarned of difficulties, as well as boons to come. These may concern physical health, or other circumstances we must deal with. It also allows us to see ourselves in an eternal light, understanding our true identity as spirit soul, not our bodies. With knowledge of our previous life's path and how to continue on our own individual spiritual journeys we can make correct choices in life to enhance this spiritual development, and also to be happy and satisfied on the material level.

The remedial measures such as gemstone therapy may be used to counteract, to a great degree, the negative planetary influences, as well as to further enhance positive planetary rays. This would then further increase benefits gained by these rays.

The goal is to be able to understand our past, present and, ultimately, future. As a result we may begin to perform actions leading to spiritual self-realisation, thus regaining our "original" consciousness. It is important to deeply contemplate the meaning of life during all stages of existence, not just to wait until death is almost upon us. By beginning to seek spiritual self-realisation early in life, individuals can develop a more elevated consciousness so that, in old age, they willfully withdraw completely from sensory objects and prepare for leaving the present body.

This is the great fault of our modern day educational system: there is no importance placed on understanding our eternal natures. Everything is geared toward attempting to gain temporary satisfaction of our bodily senses. These are destined to be finished, along with the body, in a few short years. True education is the satisfaction of our "spiritual senses" which are eternal.

I hope that the reader of this book will appreciate the light in which it was written, not only to provide some academic information, but to stimulate the "higher self" into some recognition. Yoga and meditation are the tools with which souls may uncover their eternal positions in relation to God and all other souls. This is the ultimate purpose of life, to experience "transcendental love", which fulfils our true desire, namely the connection between the individual's eternal soul and that of the Supreme Godhead.

I hope that both vedic astrologers and practitioners of ayurveda who already recommend these healing measures to their clients, as well as all western & Chinese astrologers, health care professionals, yoga students, and the general interested public will find this book useful. Furthermore, I sincerely pray that all those who read it will get a better understanding of these ancient secrets, helping them to realise the art of healing on a higher, more spiritual level.

Om Shanti Shanti Shanti.

Howard Beckman

July 1996

Hastings, England

Readers interested in the subject matter of this book may contact:

The VEDIC CULTURAL SOCIETY
6 White Rock Gardens
Hastings, E. Sussex TN34 1LD
England, U.K.

Telephone: (01424) 423019
Fax: (01424) 465398
E-mail: howard@vedastro.demon.co.uk
Websight: http://www.vedastro.demon.co.uk

SANSKRIT PRONUNCIATION GUIDE

Vowels

a	as in car
ai.	as in aisle
au	as in cow
e	as in they
i	as in sikh
o	as in so
u	as in yule

Consonants

b	as in bear
bh	as in bear/hill (pronounce letters separately)
c	as in check
ch	as in check/hill (pronounce letters separately)
d.	as in dill
dh	as in dill/hill (pronounce letters separately)
g	as in gull
gh	as in gull/hill (pronounce letters separately)
h	as in hill
j	as in jelly
jh	as in jelly/hill (pronounce letters separately)
k	as in kiln
kh	as in kiln/hill (pronounce letters separately)
l	as in load
m	as in man
n	as in new
p	as in pan
ph	as in pan/hill (pronounce letters separately)
r.	as in road
s	as in sand
sh	as in shell
t.	as in tug
th	as in tug/hill (pronounce letters separately)
v	as in volley
w	as in wash
y	as in yellow

ABOUT THE AUTHOR

Howard Beckman (Hamsavatar Das) was born and raised in Philadelphia, Pennsylvania, in a family which included both gemstone merchants and practitioners of law. Although he attended Temple University studying Philosophy and Religion his main attraction was to Eastern philosophical thought. He often visited India and was drawn to the ancient teachings of the Vedas, among them the texts on astrology and mysticism. During this time he met his spiritual master who initiated Howard into the most esoteric teachings of Bhakti-Yoga and gave him the spiritual name Hamsavatar.

After studying under some of the greatest living astrologers in India, he spent a further five years in Thailand, delving into the knowledge of precious gems and their powers to heal, one of the main remedial measures of vedic astrology to increase potentials, or lessen difficulties, in all areas of life. Upon returning to the west he further increased his knowledge by gaining a degree as a Graduate Gemologist from the Gemological Institute of America.

Howard now devotes himself full-time to teaching, lecturing, and writing about vedic sciences, and has been acclaimed for his ability to blend the knowledge and experience of Eastern and Western cultures. As a result he has become one of the most sought after speakers and personal counsellors in the astrological field worldwide. Vedic Astrology, the oldest system of astrology known to man, has been used continuously from ancient times to provide insights into peoples' lives past, present, and future. Its ultimate aim is to show our true purpose for existence, and the spiritual path we have been following for lifetimes.

Howard lives with his British wife Jennifer dividing their time between the United Kingdom, United States, and India.

BIBLIOGRAPHY

Nakshatra	Shubhakaran
Predictive Astrology of the Hindus	Pandit G.K. Ojha
Chamatkar Chintamani	Sareen
Srimad Bhagavatam	A.C. Bhaktivedanta Swami
Bhagavad Gita As It Is	A.C. Bhaktivedanta Swami
Nectar of Devotion	A.C. Bhaktivedanta Swami
Sri Chaitanya Charitamrita	A.C. Bhaktivedanta Swami
Planets in the Signs and Houses	Behari
Karmic Control Planets	M.C. Jain
How to Judge a Horoscope	B.V. Raman
Astrology of the Seers	Dr. David Frawley
Tantric Yoga and the Wisdom Goddesses	Dr. David Frawley
Ayurvedic Healing	Dr. David Frawley
How to Read Your Horoscope	Tom Hopke
Astrological Secrets of the Hebrew Sages	Dobin
An Introduction to Vedic Astrology, Spiritual Science of the Ancients	
	Howard Beckman
Gemstone Therapy for the Modern Age	Howard Beckman
Power of Tantra	Dr. N. Shrimali
Yantra	Madhu Khanna
Brihat Parasara Hora Sastra	Maharshi Parasara
Principles and Practice of Medical Astrology	Dr. Jagannath Rao
Ayurveda-the Science of Self Healing	Dr. Vasant Lad
Wealth of Susruta	Dr. K.H. Krishnamurthy
Chakras, Roots of Power	Bohm
Manual of a Mystic	Woodward
Sri Gaudiya Kanthahara	Kundali Das
Stellar Healing	N.N. Saha
The Healing Power of Gemstones	Harish Johari
Handbook of Planetary Gemology	R. Brown
Gemstones of the World	Schumann
Ancient Art of Colour Therapy	Clark
Gems and Astrology	Dr. Gouri Shanker Kapoor
Precious Stones that Heal	N.N. Saha
Collector/Investor Handbook of Gems	Ramsey
Gems and Minerals of the Bible	Wright and Chadbourne
Gem Therapy	Bhattacharya
Astrological Healing Gems	Bhattacharjee
Gemological Institute of America Gemology courses	GIA
S.R.C. Museum of Indology manuscripts	courtesy Acharya 'Vyakul'